World's Easiest
Paleo Baking

Quadruple Chocolate Cupcakes, page 163

World's Easiest

Paleo Baking

Gluten-Free, Grain-Free, Dairy-Free,
and with No Refined Sugars

· ·

Elizabeth Barbone

LAKE ISLE PRESS, NEW YORK

To Greg
Thanks for always letting me have the last cookie.

Cut-Out Cookies, page 111

Thanksgiving Pumpkin Pie, page 177

Acknowledgments

To Hiroko Kiiffner: Thank you for creating a publishing house that cares deeply about its writers. It's an honor to work with you.

To Pimpila Thanaporn: Thank you for jumping into the middle of this project with such enthusiasm and grace. Your careful editorial eye made the work shine. I'm so grateful for you.

To Jenn Sit: I'm so glad you said, "Hey, what about paleo baking?" This book happened because of you. Thank you.

To my readers and online friends: Thank you for your friendship. I deeply cherish our wonderful community and all the friendships that have formed because of it. And thank you for cheering for this book from the very beginning.

To my mother, Chris Barbone: Thank you for everything. During this project you washed dishes, ran countless trips to the grocery store, and created backdrops for the photography. Most of all, you were a constant source of love and encouragement. I'm so incredibly lucky that you're my mom.

To Greg: When I told you Jenn said, "Hey, what about paleo baking?" You replied, "Yes! Do it!" Thank you for your unwavering support, not only during this project but in everything I do. Together we dare greatly. I love you.

Published by:
Lake Isle Press, Inc.
2095 Broadway, Suite 301
New York, NY 10023
(212) 273-0796
E-mail: info@lakeislepress.com

Distributed to the trade by:
National Book Network, Inc.
4501 Forbes Boulevard, Suite 200
Lanham, MD 20706
1(800) 462-6420
www.nbnbooks.com

Library of Congress Control Number: 2015952912

ISBN-13: 978-1-891105-57-9
ISBN-10: 1-891105-57-4

Book and cover design: Liz Trovato
Editor: Pimpila Thanaporn

This book is available at special sales discounts for bulk purchases
as premiums or special editions, including customized covers.
For more information, contact the publisher at
(212) 273-0796 or by e-mail: info@lakeislepress.com

First edition
Printed in the USA

10 9 8 7 6 5 4 3 2 1

Contents

Introduction

Thirty years later and I still remember the whoopie pie.

I was six or seven at the time, though my age isn't as clear in my memory as the dark chocolate cakes sandwiched together with a bright white filling. My friend Tiffany's mom had baked whoopie pies while Tiffany and I played with our Cabbage Patch dolls. I'd never seen a whoopie pie. Cannoli and sfogliatelle, sure, those were normal desserts around our house. A giant, soft sandwich cookie–looking thing? This was new to me. And I wanted it. Badly.

Then I asked the dreaded question: "Am I allergic to this?"

My friend's mom froze. She'd obviously forgotten about my allergies. So she picked up the phone—cream-colored, with a rotary dial—and called my mother. As she stood there twirling the phone cord around her finger, I willed my mother to pick up. She didn't. That meant one thing: no whoopie pie for me.

Tiffany ate hers with gusto, crumbs and frosting sticking to her face, while I watched. I'm sure her mother gave me a snack. I don't remember what it was. An hour or so later my mother arrived and I started to ask about the whoopie pie. My mom shushed me and said it was too close to dinner for a snack. I was crushed.

Over the years, I've experienced lots of whoopie pie moments—times when something looked so good . . . only I couldn't eat it. Despite my allergies, I loved new foods and spending time in the kitchen with my mother. She was my first cooking teacher. After high school, I headed to The Culinary Institute of America. I took everything I learned and applied it to gluten-free and allergen-friendly baking.

After writing two gluten-free cookbooks and teaching countless cooking classes, I felt totally at home with gluten-free baking. My allergies were managed, so I didn't expect to change the way I baked or ate.

And then . . . I met Michelle.

About two years ago, I sat in a little boat at Walt Disney World with Michelle Tam—online she goes by the adorable moniker Nom Nom Paleo. We were at Disney for a food bloggers' conference.

As the boat moved slowly through the water, we talked about the paleo diet. I wasn't really familiar with it. Wasn't that the one where people only ate meat? Michelle clarified: No, it wasn't just meat. She told me that she avoided gluten and grains but ate lots of vegetables, fruit, and other interesting foods—including, yes, meat.

Michelle said that she didn't eat much in the way of baked goods but that some people who followed a paleo diet did. We talked about gluten-free baking (my specialty) and I admitted that I had no idea how you'd bake without grains. Privately I was thinking, "No rice? Or corn? Or sorghum? What??!?"

Our conversation stayed with me. It seemed like overnight, requests for grain-free recipes filled my in-box. Some folks ate grain-free due to allergies, some for autoimmune issues, and others just felt that a grain-free diet was the best fit for their body. The people reaching out to me had one thing in common—they all wanted baked treats.

I thought about that whoopie pie from years ago. How it felt to want it so much but not be able to eat it.

Into the kitchen I went. I wanted to give grain-free, paleo baking a try. It sounded downright impossible. At first it was. My cakes were too dense, cookies too hard. And coconut flour flummoxed me. Whenever I felt down about it—you know, when a recipe flopped—I'd glance at the Susan B. Anthony magnet on my refrigerator that says "Failure Is Impossible." At those moments, failure looked possible. But I figured Susan B. knew what she was talking about so I tried again.

The first recipe that worked, really worked, was a simple yellow cake. The recipe was free of grains, dairy, and refined sugars. It was a success worth celebrating! So I did—with a piece of cake.

Over time, I taught myself how to bake well without grains. I made cookies, cakes, pies, hearty baguettes, and—of course—whoopie pies. So that *you* can make cookies, cakes, pies, and hearty baguettes, too.

Some people believe that living grain-free means living without baked goods. I respect that choice.

However, if you live grain-free and want to enjoy the occasional treat, this book is for you.

These recipes require some special ingredients, like almond and coconut flours, but the techniques are easy enough for even the shyest baker.

Happy Paleo Baking!

Elizabeth Barbone

FAQs

Who is this book for?

Anyone! If you follow a grain-free diet, a paleo diet, eat grain-free from time to time, or are just looking for some new and tasty recipes, this book is for you.

Why grain-free baked goods?
People eat grain-free for many different reasons. Some follow a grain-free diet due to allergies or other health concerns, like autoimmune disorders. Some eat grain-free because they feel better without grains. And others eat grain-free just because. It doesn't matter why you eat grain-free, there's a place for you at my table!

Baked treats did not exist in Paleolithic times. So don't grain-free baked goods go against the philosophy of grain-free diets?
The answer depends on the diet you follow. Some grain-free and paleo diets don't include baked goods. But if you follow a grain-free diet and enjoy an occasional treat, these recipes are for you.

How do grain-free baked goods differ from ones made with grains?
Treats made without grains vary a little from those made with them. The batters are thicker. Cakes and muffins are a little denser. Breads don't rise as high. But the taste? Oh, wow. Almond flour and coconut flour are flavor powerhouses. Over time, I began to prefer the more flavorful, less sweet grain-free treats to ones made with grain.

Are these recipes gluten-free?
Yes. All recipes in the book are gluten-free.

Are the recipes sugar-free?
No. The recipes use unrefined sugars like maple syrup, honey, coconut sugar, and evaporated cane juice. The sugar content in the recipes is kept low while still providing enough sweetness. (For more information on sugar in baking, see page 15.)

Are the recipes gum-free?
Yes. None of the recipes contain xanthan gum or guar gum.

Are the recipes dairy-free?
All recipes in the book can be made dairy-free. If your diet does include dairy, dairy options are included throughout the book.

Are the recipes egg-free?
No. Eggs are used throughout the book.

Aren't eggs dairy?
Nope! Dairy comes from the mammary glands of mammals. (Some common examples: cow's milk, goat's milk, buffalo's milk.) Eggs come from poultry.

Are you sure?
Yes. I'm sure. Eggs are not dairy.

What about baking powder? Powdered sugar?
Baking powder and powdered sugar usually contain a grain-based starch, most commonly, cornstarch. To make them at home, see page 210. If you don't want to make them at home, see Sources (page 211) for where to order grain-free versions.

Where do I begin?
I'd suggest starting with anything except the baguette or pie crust recipes, which are more advanced.

How do I stock my grain-free pantry?
Here are some basics:

> Almond flour
> Coconut flour
> Baking soda
> Cream of tartar (to make your own baking powder)
> Dark maple syrup
> Honey
> Coconut sugar
> Evaporated cane juice
> Coconut oil
> Eggs
> Milk, dairy-free, or traditional (if your diet includes dairy)
> Unsalted butter (if your diet includes dairy)

For more information on ingredients, see following page.

Ingredients

Grain-Free? Then What the Heck Do I Bake With?!?

Before I started baking without grains, I didn't have a clue how someone could do it. What's included? What's off limits? Maybe you are just as confused. Here's my handy-dandy chart of what's used and what's not.

Ingredients Used in This Book	Ingredients Not Used in This Book
Flours Almond Coconut	**Flours** Wheat Rye Barley Oat Rice (brown, white, and sweet) Sorghum Cornmeal, corn flour
Starches Tapioca starch	**Starches** Cornstarch Potato starch Wheat starch
Sweeteners Dark maple syrup Honey Coconut sugar Granulated maple sugar Evaporated cane juice	**Sweeteners** Refined sugar Stevia Artificial sweeteners Corn syrup
Fats Coconut oil Olive oil Grapeseed oil Palm shortening Unsalted butter* Lard**	**Fats** Margarine Soy-based shortening Liquid vegetable oil (soybean, corn, canola)
Dairy-Free or Dairy Options Coconut milk Almond milk Traditional milk* Half-and-half Heavy cream	**Dairy-Free or Dairy Options** Cheese Yogurt Soy milk

*If your diet includes dairy   **If your diet includes pork

Flours and Starches

The one thing grain-filled and grain-free flours have in common is that they are essential to providing structure and flavor to baked goods. Apart from that, grain-free flours behave very differently. To succeed in the kitchen, it's important to know the specific properties of each kind. The easiest mistake is to use the wrong flour. Swapping the same amount of coconut flour for almond flour will almost surely give you a flop. Here's a handy guide to how the different flours behave and the important benefits they bring to recipes.

Almond Flour

Made from finely ground blanched almonds, almond flour imparts a delicate flavor and texture to baked goods. It's high in fat, so you'll notice that recipes using mostly almond flour have little or no additional fat or oil added to them.

When selecting almond flour, look for bags marked "finely ground" or even "super finely ground." You want to avoid coarsely ground almond flour and the even coarser almond meal. Recipes made with almond meal sometimes don't work as directed and bake up very gritty. I order my almond flour online from Honeyville.com or Nuts.com.

For times when you want a break from almond flour, replace it with an equal amount of hazelnut flour, cashew flour, or sunflower seed flour. (Just note that baked goods made with sunflower seed flour and baking powder or baking soda tend to turn green-blue due to a reaction between the natural chlorophyll in the flour and the sodium bicarbonate. They are safe to eat but will look weird. Really weird.)

BAKER'S NOTE: *I want to save money. Should I make my own almond flour?*

While you can make your own by grinding blanched almonds in a blender or food processor, I don't recommend it. It's hard to get a superfine grind in a home blender, even a high-powered one like a Blendtec or Vitamix. When trying to get a fine enough grind, you often end up tipping over into almond butter. While almond butter is great (yum!), it's not almond flour.

Coconut Flour

Made from dried defatted coconut meat, coconut flour is high in fiber. It adds a light, cake-like texture to baked goods. Coconut flour absorbs more water than any other flour I've ever worked with, and in recipes where it's the primary flour, you'll notice a high ratio of liquids (like eggs) to flour. This is normal.

Thick batters are also normal with coconut flour. Cake batter so thick you can stand a wooden spoon up in it? Normal. Using just a little flour for a full batch of cookies or muffins? Yup, that's normal, too.

Be sure to purchase coconut flour made from dried defatted coconut meat. You don't want dried coconut (sometimes labeled "desiccated coconut"), which doesn't work the same in baking recipes.

Coconut flours often vary in color from light, creamy beige to dark tan. This is normal and varies brand to brand and batch to batch. While they all work in recipes, you might prefer one brand over another. Experiment to find the one you love. (Note: If you have celiac disease, buy a gluten free coconut flour. Some brands carry "may contain" warnings for wheat/gluten.)

Unique in every way, no other flour works like it.

BAKER'S NOTE: *Can I make my own coconut flour?*
No. Making your own from unsweetened dried coconut doesn't work like defatted coconut flour, and the recipe will flop.

Tapioca Starch

Tapioca starch is a white, powdery starch extracted from the South American cassava plant. It adds elasticity and lightness to baked goods like breads and cakes. With tapioca starch, you can knead the pasta dough and several other recipes in this book. Without it, a kneadable dough is hard, if not impossible, to achieve.

For baking, you want tapioca starch (sometimes labeled "tapioca flour"), not tapioca pearls or granules.

Some people detect a slight metallic taste in some brands, though no one seems to agree on which ones. What tastes good to you might taste metallic to someone else. If it tastes subtly metallic to you, switch brands. That usually solves the problem.

If you need to avoid tapioca starch, replace it with another starch, not almond or coconut flour. I suggest using arrowroot starch, which is more expensive than tapioca starch but works about the same. Arrowroot starch doesn't provide as much "stretch," so it's best to use it as a substitute in recipes that call for less than ½ cup. The finished recipe might be a little denser. I don't recommend using arrowroot starch if the recipe calls for kneading (e.g., pasta or bread dough) because it doesn't provide the same elastic properties.

Sugars

Ah, sugar. While creating the recipes for this book, I thought a lot about sugar. And I trust that you, too, have thought a lot about it.

I'm a baker, not a doctor or dietitian. So I want to talk about sugar from a baking point of view. Before I do, I'll just say that I developed all the recipes to keep sugar to a minimum, though it's a good idea to limit your overall sugar intake and to keep treats, like the ones found in this book, to occasional indulgences.

From a nutrition standpoint, sugar is sugar. All those claims about some sugars containing extra nutrients are, to me, a little misleading. There are trace nutrients in unrefined sugar, that's true. However, you'd have to eat so much of those sugars to get any nutritional benefit that you'd make yourself sick, which kind of defeats the purpose.

My body and my baking don't do well with sweeteners like stevia or xylitol. And my body especially dislikes artificial sweeteners. This means that you'll find only natural, unrefined sugar used throughout the book. Most of the recipes call for maple syrup, honey, coconut sugar, granulated maple sugar, or evaporated cane juice. A few call for unsulphured molasses.

Why unrefined sugars? Flavor. Regular white table sugar? Meh. It tastes sweet. That's it. Maple sugar and coconut sugar, on the other hand, bring flavor to baked goods.

On top of adding flavor and sweetness, sugar plays many important roles in baking. It helps feed yeast, acts as a preservative in foods like jams, aerates cakes, delays crystallization in candy making, adds color to baked goods, and does much more. Since sugar attracts and retains moisture

(it's hygroscopic), it keeps baked goods moist and delays staling.

That's a lot, right?

As you can imagine, omitting or changing the type or amount of sugar called for in a recipe will affect the outcome. Totally omitting the sugar from a recipe will cause it to fail. If you prefer one sugar to another, however, feel free to swap. Just remember to swap a liquid sugar, like honey, for another liquid sugar, like maple syrup. And the same goes for dry sugars. For more information on substitutions, check the descriptions of specific sugars below.

Dry Sugars

Coconut Sugar

Made from the nectar of coconut palm blossoms, coconut sugar tastes mildly nutty with some hints of caramel. It's an unrefined sugar, so the color and flavor vary from batch to batch. Because it acts like cane sugar, it's ideal for baking.

If you don't like the flavor of coconut sugar, substitute it 1:1 with evaporated cane juice or granulated maple sugar. You can also use half coconut sugar and half evaporated cane juice or maple sugar for a milder flavor. Don't replace coconut sugar with a liquid sugar like maple syrup or honey.

Evaporated Cane Juice

Evaporated cane juice (sometimes labeled "organic cane sugar") is less refined than white granulated sugar, which can be made from either cane sugar or beet sugar. Evaporated cane juice has a golden hue and a flavor that varies from light caramel to strong molasses.

You want evaporated cane juice to look like small sugar crystals. If the brand you buy contains large pieces or lumps, give it a quick spin in your blender or food processor. You don't want to blend it so long that you make powdered sugar but just enough to break up the clumps. In my Blendtec, this takes about 5 seconds on low speed. In my Cuisinart food processor, this takes about four long pulses.

If your diet doesn't include evaporated cane sugar, replace it 1:1 with coconut sugar or granulated maple sugar. Don't replace evaporated cane juice with liquid sugars like honey or maple syrup.

BAKER'S NOTE: *How about Sucanat and muscovado?*

Good question! Both are cane sugars, but different from each other. Somewhat.

Sucanat is a registered trademark. The name comes from SUgar CAne NATural. (See what they did there? Clever!) Sucanat is dried cane juice with a very strong molasses flavor. The texture is like very tiny pebbles instead of sugar crystals. While it can be used as a 1:1 replacement for evaporated cane juice, I don't recommend it because the flavor can overpower delicate baked goods.

Muscovado is sugar with the molasses left in. Unlike traditional brown sugar, which is refined sugar with molasses added back in, muscovado usually doesn't have the molasses removed in the first place, although this varies from producer to producer. It's a very damp sugar and isn't recommended as a substitute for the sugars in this book.

Granulated Maple Sugar

Maple sugar is made by boiling pure maple syrup until all the water is removed. The boiled syrup is then cooled, ground, and sifted. It has a very fine texture and a strong maple flavor.

Maple sugar isn't cheap! If your budget or your taste buds don't like it, substitute it 1:1 with coconut sugar or evaporated cane juice. Just don't replace granulated maple sugar with maple syrup (or honey, for that matter). Maple syrup and honey contain water, which affects the recipes.

Powdered Sugar

Powdered sugar is a finely ground sugar. Typically it's made from a refined sugar with a starch added to prevent clumping. Sometimes it's called "confectioners' sugar." When selecting, look for one that contains a grain-free starch (see Sources, page 211) or make your own (page 210). I use powdered sugar in frosting and marzipan.

There's no substitute for it. Its soft texture is needed whenever it's called for in this book.

Liquid Sugars

Honey

Bees take nectar from flowers and turn it into honey. Amazing. As of this writing, there's growing evidence that many commercial brands of honey aren't 100 percent pure. Many contain corn syrup or other sweeteners. To avoid adulterated honey, buy from local producers. Be sure to purchase liquid, not creamed, honey.

For a honey substitute, replace with an equal amount of maple syrup or use half maple syrup and half honey (the blend tastes like light caramel to me).

BAKER'S NOTE: *Help! My honey crystalized!*

Honey crystallization is fairly common. Here's what to do when it happens:

- **Fill a small saucepan with enough water to cover the honey jar halfway.**
- **Heat the water to about 95°F, no hotter than 106°F.**
- **Turn off the heat; if you have an electric stovetop, remove the pan from the heat.**
- **Remove the lid from the jar and place the jar in the water.**
- **Stir occasionally until the honey is liquid. This takes about 30 minutes.**

Maple Syrup

Maple syrup is made by boiling the sap of sugar maple trees. The flavor of the syrup varies by color. Darker syrups are more flavorful than lighter-colored ones. According to Cornell Sugar Maple Research and Extension: "Syrup flavor is affected by soil type, tree genetics, weather conditions during the maple season, time during the season when the sap is collected, and processing technique." I love that the flavor varies by year and producer. Try a few different brands to see which you enjoy. And remember, next year, the flavor might be different. This is totally normal!

Some folks believe that darker syrups contain more impurities and are less refined than lighter ones. This isn't true. Syrups are graded based on color, not impurities. All grades are the same quality, and will perform the same in baking.

For baking recipes, purchase dark maple syrup. Up until recently, this was called "Grade B." Dark maple syrup has a robust flavor that comes through in baked goods. If you don't want an intense maple flavor, look for a lighter-colored syrup, usually labeled "golden" or "amber." Be sure to avoid maple-flavored syrup or pancake syrup,

which are not the real thing and often contain corn syrup.

If you live in an area that produces maple syrup, buy from a local source. Otherwise, check out Dakin Farm, Whole Foods, or Trader Joe's (see Sources, page 211).

You can replace maple syrup with an equal amount of honey or use half honey and half maple syrup. The finished baked good won't be as dark and will taste a little different, but it will work—and I love the flavor!

Molasses

Molasses is a byproduct of the sugar-making process, made by boiling the liquid that's left after the sugar cane has been crushed. The liquid can be boiled three times. With each boiling, the syrup gets darker and more robust, yielding three types: light (mild), dark (robust), and blackstrap. I bake with light or dark molasses because I find the flavor of blackstrap molasses overpowering.

If you don't care for the flavor of molasses, replace it with equal parts honey or maple syrup. They are lighter in flavor and color than molasses, so the taste of the baked good will change, but it will work.

Fats and Oils

After years of being told to avoid it at all costs, we are starting to rethink fats. Thank goodness, because fats are a baking superhero! Think I'm overstating? Try baking a cake without coating the pan with oil. Or make a batch of cookies and omit the fat. You know what you'll get? A cake that's stuck in the pan and cookies that are dry and tasteless. Who wants that?

In baking, like flours and sugars, fat plays multiple roles. It keeps cakes moist, adds a flaky texture to piecrust, makes for creamy frosting, and brings flavor to recipes.

Here is a guide to different types of fat, how they're used, and what role they play in baking.

Solid Fats

Coconut Oil

Coconut oil is made by extracting the fat from coconut meat. It's a great replacement for butter and vegetable shortening in paleo baking. Some brands taste strongly of coconut; others do not.

You want to purchase a coconut oil that's solid

at cool temperatures (76°F or below) and liquid when warmer. I prefer organic, virgin cold-pressed coconut oil.

Don't buy "liquid coconut oil," which has been manufactured to remain a liquid, even at cool temperatures. It will be clearly labeled as such or "fractionated coconut oil" or "MCT (medium-chain triglyceride) coconut oil." It does not behave the same as traditional coconut oil in baking.

If your diet includes dairy, feel free to replace the coconut oil with unsalted butter. If you eat dairy-free and need a coconut oil substitute, reach for leaf lard or palm shortening (I recommended palm shortening with hesitation; see more on following page). It's important to swap coconut oil with another fat of the same texture. That means if a recipe calls for solid coconut oil, you want to use softened butter or solid palm shortening. Likewise, if the recipe calls for melted coconut oil, you want to use melted butter, lard, or palm shortening.

BAKER'S NOTE: *Coconut Oil Temperature Matters*

The texture of fats is important in baking. Solid fats help to leaven cookies and make pastry flaky, and using a liquid fat in place of a solid fat dramatically changes the final product.

Coconut oil changes texture depending on its temperature. Below 76°F, it's a solid. Above 76°F, it's a liquid. When a recipe calls for solid coconut oil, you want the oil white and creamy. If you stick your finger or a spoon into it, it should offer slight resistance. You don't want the oil so cold that it's brittle. If it's cold in your kitchen, pop the coconut oil in the microwave on low heat for about 15 seconds to warm. You want to soften it slightly, not melt it.

In the summer, if your coconut oil turns to liquid, chill it for about an hour before you plan to bake. I don't recommend storing coconut oil in the refrigerator because it gets rock hard. If you do store your coconut oil in the fridge, allow it to soften before you bake, or heat it in the microwave for a few seconds.

BAKER'S NOTE: *What's the difference between coconut oil and coconut butter?*

Coconut oil and coconut butter sound like they are the same thing, don't they? And to confuse matters even further, they look alike. But they aren't the same, and in recipes, using the wrong one spells disaster.

Coconut oil is a pure fat, extracted from coconut meat; think of this like almond oil. Coconut butter is made by grinding coconut meat; think of this like almond butter. Imagine trying to sauté with a dab of almond butter instead of almond oil and you'll understand why the two are not interchangeable. You can't extract coconut oil at home, but you can make coconut butter if you own a high-powered blender or food processor. For a recipe, see page 205.

Butter and Ghee

Rich and delicate, butter bakes up wonderfully. If your diet includes dairy, reach for unsalted butter when baking. (I like grass-fed butter, but that's a preference, not a requirement.)

Ghee is a type of clarified butter made by gently boiling unsalted butter. The natural water content evaporates and the milk proteins settle to the bottom. The butter is strained to remove those milk solids, and you're left with pure butterfat. Ghee is solid at room temperature and usually bright yellow. It can be used in baking, but like other substitutions, results will vary. In some recipes, like pie crust, it works very well. In other recipes, like cookies, sometimes you are left with a heavier, almost greasy cookie. If you prefer ghee to butter, give it a try but know that the results will vary from recipe to recipe.

BAKER'S NOTE: *Butter Temperature Matters*

Like coconut oil, butter is affected by temperature. You'll see three butter temperatures called for in the recipes.

Chilled: About 38°F, this is straight-from-the-refrigerator butter. It's cold and brittle. Use this butter in pie crust recipes or any other time you need to cut cold fat into flour.

Softened: Between 65° and 68°F, butter is soft and creamy. At this temperature, the butter should give easily when poked, but it should not be melted at all.

To quickly soften butter, place it in a large plastic bag and hit it with a rolling pin until soft. (This technique also works well as stress reducer.)

Melted: At about 90°F, butter melts. Melt butter in the microwave (use a low-heat setting to prevent the butter from splattering all over the inside of your microwave) or in a small saucepan over low heat. Don't heat the butter so much that the milk solids turn brown. (While browned butter is tasty, it's not called for in any recipe in this book.)

After the butter melts, allow it to cool slightly before adding it to the recipe.

Lard

Lard is pig fat. It's white, creamy, and delicious. If your diet includes pork, give it a try. It's lovely in pie crust and in frosting. Lard softens faster than other fats. If it's warm in your kitchen, keep the lard in the refrigerator until you're ready to use it.

Look for "leaf lard," the highest quality of lard and the most pure tasting. If you can't find it, look for pasture-raised pure lard. Always avoid hydrogenated lard, which is a hydrogenated fat and often contains other additives.

Palm Shortening

For times when you need to avoid coconut, dairy, and lard, palm shortening is a good choice. I use Spectrum Natural's Organic Shortening. It's non-hydrogenated and works well in pie crusts and frosting recipes. In other recipes, like cakes and cookies, palm shortening can add a bit of a plastic mouthfeel. Only use shortening when other fats aren't an option.

The harvesting of palm oil can be problematic, leading to deforestation and harm to animals, including the orangutan. If you select palm shortening, be sure to purchase it from a reputable and sustainable source.

Liquid Oils

Almond Oil

Almond oil has a delicate flavor, and it works well for sautéing and baking. If you don't eat almonds, replace it with a mild-flavored olive oil or grapeseed oil.

Grapeseed Oil

Grapeseed oil is a byproduct of the winemaking industry, made from the seeds of grapes. The oil has a neutral flavor, which makes it great for baking. If you can't find it, replace it with almond oil or olive oil.

Nonstick Cooking Spray

Nonstick cooking spray is great for greasing cake pans. It is often made from grain-based oils, so look for one made from coconut oil. Be sure to avoid any that contain wheat, like Baker's Joy. If you don't want to use a cooking spray, brush pans lightly with melted coconut oil to prevent cakes and other baked goods from sticking.

Olive Oil

The flavor of olive oil varies depending on the quality. For all of the recipes in this book, I recommend regular olive oil. It has a delicate flavor that doesn't overpower the recipe the way extra-virgin olive oil can. If you don't like olive oil, replace it with almond or grapeseed oil.

Leaveners

Leaveners help baked goods rise by introducing gas bubbles to batters and doughs. There are two types of leaveners: chemical (baking powder and soda) and biological (yeast). If you forget the leavening, a baked good will turn out dense and heavy.

Baking Soda

Baking soda (sodium bicarbonate) is an alkali that, by itself, has no leavening power. It must combine with an acid, like lemon juice, natural cocoa powder, or molasses, to release carbon dioxide, which causes batters to rise. There's no replacement for baking soda. Be sure to always have a fresh box on hand. If your baking soda contains clumps, sift it before using.

Baking Powder

When I started baking without grains, I almost shouted, "Oh, c'mon! Baking powder too?!?!" Yup. Most commercial baking powders contain grain, usually cornstarch, which prevents the baking powder from clumping. If you follow a strict grain-free diet or have corn allergies, make your own grain-free version (page 210) or purchase one (see Sources, page 211). All recipes in this book were tested with homemade baking powder. Commercial ones tend to thicken batter slightly more. If you use commercial baking powder and your batter looks too thick, add a small (one tablespoon or so) amount of liquid, like milk or water, to thin it out.

Unlike baking soda, baking powder contains its own acid. This means it only requires the presence of a liquid to produce carbon dioxide. To test the

potency of baking powder, spoon about a teaspoon into a small cup. Add a splash of water. If it bubbles and fizzes, it's good to use.

BAKER'S NOTE: *Single Acting vs. Double Acting. Why is baking powder so dramatic?*

Pick up a can of most baking powders and you'll notice the words "double acting." Sounds a little like a high school drama club, doesn't it?

Double-acting baking powder contains two acids, a base (usually sodium bicarbonate), and a starch. It reacts first when liquid causes the acids and base to combine, and again when exposed to heat. This means that commercial baking powder releases some bubbles (carbon dioxide, actually) when you add liquid to the batter. It can be any liquid—water, dairy-free milk, eggs, etc. Then when you slide the pan into the oven, it releases more bubbles.

For the baker, double-acting baking powder is like an insurance policy. If you leave the batter on your counter for too long, you get a second chance for a rise when it goes into the oven.

Homemade baking powder is single acting: It only reacts in the bowl. If you leave your bowl of batter sitting around for too long, those bubbles can pop and leave you with a flat baked good. No one wants that! The insurance policy for homemade single-acting baking powder is a simple one: Don't forget to preheat your oven. That's it.

With a preheated oven, you mix your batter, pop it in the pan, and bake. The bubbles in your batter won't have a chance to pop. This isn't something to stress about. You just want to be aware that your cakes and muffins and other goodies won't rise in the oven if you wait too long.

Yeast

Humans have used yeast to leaven bread for centuries. Yeast feeds on the carbohydrates (sugar and starch) in dough and produces carbon dioxide that makes the dough rise. Cool, eh?

You'll find three varieties of yeast available at the supermarket: instant, active dry, and fresh (cake) yeast. I recommend instant yeast or active dry. Unlike dried yeast, fresh yeast has a very short life, and in my experience, it doesn't work well.

Unlike chemical leaveners, yeast is a living organism, and it needs a little bit of special handling to work. (The good news for the baker is that commercial yeast is a fairly reliable product. So don't let it make you nervous!)

When working with yeast, keep these things in mind.

1. Check the expiration date. You want the yeast to be fresh.
2. Don't use hot water. It's better if your water is too cool than too hot. The ideal temperature is between 100° and 110°F.
3. Don't add salt directly to the yeast-water mixture. When in direct contact, salt can kill the yeast.
4. Don't add too much sugar to the yeast-water mixture. About 1 teaspoon will tell you if the yeast is active; the mixture should bubble about 10 minutes after you add the sugar. Any more than 1 teaspoon of sugar can kill the yeast.

Traditional Milk and Dairy-Free Alternatives

Dairy ranks right up there with sugar as a class of food that folks differ on. Some people who follow a paleo or grain-free diet don't eat dairy. Some do. Others avoid dairy for medical reasons. Some can handle a little, others a lot.

What's a cookbook author to do? Well, in this case, it's pretty easy. If your diet includes dairy, substitute ingredients like unsalted butter and traditional milk for the dairy-free ingredients such as coconut oil and coconut milk called for in a recipe. Throughout the book, you'll find the substitutions listed like this:

57 grams (¼ cup) coconut oil, solid, or unsalted butter, softened

226 grams (1 cup) milk, dairy-free or traditional

Select the best dairy or dairy-free ingredient that works for you.

Dairy adds flavor and color to baked goods. Cookies made with butter might spread a little more than cookies made with coconut oil. Other than that, you shouldn't notice any big changes in a recipe.

Coconut Milk and Coconut Cream

Coconut milk is the liquid obtained by pureeing coconut meat with water, then straining out the solids. Don't confuse it with sweetened cream of coconut, which is used for mixed drinks, not baking.

There are a variety of coconut milks available on the market. I prefer full-fat coconut milk, though reduced-fat versions will work in recipes unless otherwise noted. If you use full-fat coconut milk, be sure to whisk the milk until smooth before using it in a recipe.

For recipes calling for coconut cream, chill the can, then scoop off the fat. (You can drink the leftover clear coconut milk or use it in a smoothie.)

Traditional Milk and Cream

If your diet includes dairy, use cow's milk wherever traditional milk is listed as an option. Some recipes specify half-and-half or heavy cream. I buy local milk. In fact, I always have at least one glass bottle clanging around in the backseat of my car waiting to be returned to Battenkill Valley Creamery. If local milk isn't an option, I suggest buying organic.

Almond Milk

You can use almond milk in most recipes where "milk, dairy-free or traditional" is called for. It will not work where a cream-like milk is needed, like whipped coconut cream or The World's Easiest (and Richest!) Chocolate Pie (page 181).

Other Ingredients

Eggs

Eggs are an important part of grain-free baking, and you'll find that many recipes, especially those made with coconut flour, call for more eggs than their grain-filled counterparts. Eggs are essential because they bring structure to baked goods. They don't replace gluten—there's nothing quite like it—but they do help cakes and breads rise while providing flavor and color.

Whenever a recipe calls for eggs, use large ones that weigh about 50 grams each. If you're like me and you buy local eggs, remember to weigh your eggs (out of the shell, please) before adding them to a recipe. The size of non-factory-produced eggs tends to vary and a "large" egg from a local hen might be smaller than one from a grocery store. Each recipe includes the weight for eggs. Don't go crazy trying to get it down to the gram. A variance of 5 grams either way is fine.

While there are many egg replacers, like flax meal and chia, available for people with egg allergies, none of the recipes have been tested without eggs. If you are egg-free, and have an egg replacer you love, give it a try. I recommend starting with recipes that use two eggs or less—when a recipe contains more than that, it can be very difficult to get a successful result.

Salt

Don't think small changes in recipes matter? Go ahead and leave out that ½ teaspoon salt and you'll see that even the tiniest ingredient makes a big difference in baking. Salt enhances flavor in baked goods and keeps yeast under control. This is important; if too much yeast growth occurs, a bread can rise too high and then collapse. Controlled yeast growth is a good thing.

There's a bit of a salt-mania happening right now in food: Smoked salt. Pink salt. Red salt. Heck, I just ate black salt the other day. (It was awesome!) All of these choices are great for cooking. Not for baking, though. Except for a few recipes that call for kosher salt, use fine-grained table salt because it blends easily into batters. It's up to you whether you want to use iodized or not.

Chocolate

Chocolate Bars

There's nothing quite like a piece of good chocolate. The flavor of chocolate varies from producer to producer depending on the source, the amount of cocoa butter it contains, and how it was processed. What tastes good to me might not taste as good to you. If you don't already have a favorite chocolate bar, try a few different ones (hard work, I know!) until you find one that you love. Look for a soy and dairy-free dark chocolate with 72% cacao content or higher. Recipes like truffles made with a lower percentage of cacao won't set up correctly.

Chocolate Chips or Chunks

Most chocolate chips contain dairy and soy lecithin, so check the ingredients list and look for a dairy-free, soy-free brand. I like Enjoy Life dark chocolate morsels. If you are unable to find them, chop a dairy-free, soy-free chocolate bar into small, bite-size pieces and use that in its place. I like to keep mini and regular chips and chunks in the pantry—they are great for cookies and frosting.

Don't use chocolate chips for truffles or any recipe that calls for chocolate with a specific percentage of cacao. Most chocolate chips don't contain enough cocoa butter to make truffles and other chocolate treats.

Cocoa Powder

Cocoa powder is made from pulverized roasted cocoa beans. There are two types of cocoa powder on the market: natural and Dutch-process. Natural cocoa powder is naturally acidic and light in color. The acid reacts with baking soda in a recipe to leaven baked goods.

Dutch-process cocoa is treated with a potassium solution to neutralize the acidity. It's very dark in color and has a strong chocolate flavor. Since the acid has been neutralized, baking powder needs to be added to leaven recipes.

BAKER'S NOTE: *Is it okay to swap natural and Dutch-process cocoa powders?*

There are times when it doesn't matter which cocoa powder you use, and there are times when it does. Both natural or Dutch-process cocoa powder work in puddings, frosting, hot cocoa, and sauces. But in recipes where there's baking soda or baking powder, it matters which kind you use. Since natural cocoa powder is acidic, it works better in recipes that use baking soda. Dutch-process cocoa powder has had its acid neutralized, so it requires baking powder for leavening. All recipes in this book specify which to use.

BAKER'S NOTE: *Storage Time for Recipes*

You'll see storage times for many of the recipes in the book. Think of these as gentle suggestions. Grain-free recipes tend to stale faster than their grain-filled counterparts, and humidity affects them in a big way. When the environment is dry, things dry out—you'll notice this especially with cakes. When it's humid, things get moist—you'll notice crisp cookies turn soft. If a recipe states that you can store something on the counter for a few days and you notice that the quality is going downhill, wrap the leftovers well and pop them in the freezer.

BAKER'S NOTE: *How to Freeze Baked Goods*

Baked goods are best enjoyed within a day or so of baking. One of the best ways to store baked goods is to freeze them. Here's how:

1. Allow them to cool completely. Freezing warm baked goods adversely affects the texture.
2. Tightly wrap the cooled baked goods with plastic wrap. Then wrap again. This prevents freezer burn.
3. Finally, wrap in heavy-duty aluminum foil and label and date your baked goods.

Specific freezing time for most baked goods can be found in the recipes. And, in the few cases where recipes don't freeze well, I've made a note.

Kitchen Tools

You probably already own most of the tools needed to make the recipes in this book. Here's what I suggest having on hand.

Hand Tools

Balloon Whisk

Look for a whisk with long, thin loops of stainless steel that connect at the handle. Pick one that feels good in your hand. I use an 8-inch balloon whisk (the most common style). Avoid roux whisks (sometimes called "flat whisks"), spiral whisks, cage whisks that contain a small ball in the center of the loops, and whisks with unjoined tines. None of these whisks does a good job for the recipes in this book.

Citrus Zester

Citrus zest adds a lovely kick of flavor to recipes. You want only the thin, bright skin of the fruit, not the bitter white pith right under it. I use a Microplane zester for superfine zest. If you are using a traditional zester, it will yield long strips of zest that you should chop before adding to the recipe.

Measuring Cups

There are two different styles of measuring cups: one for liquids and another for dry ingredients. You need both styles—they are not interchangeable. It's inaccurate to measure dry ingredients in a liquid measuring cup because you can't level the ingredient, resulting in either too much or too little flour. As for measuring a liquid in a dry measuring cup, you can do it but I don't recommend it because you have to fill the cup to the brim and you might spill some of the liquid before it gets into your bowl.

Liquid Measuring Cups

Usually made of glass or plastic with a handle and spout, liquid measuring cups are used to measure ingredients like water, milk, honey, and maple syrup. I prefer a glass 2-cup liquid measure.

Nested Dry Measuring Cups

To measure flour, starches, and dry sugars, look for a set of metal nested dry measuring cups that include ¼-cup to 1-cup measures.

BAKER'S NOTE: *How to Use a Dry Measuring Cup*

Let's say you don't own a kitchen scale. I recommend buying a kitchen scale ASAP. But in the meantime . . . I still want you to be able to bake. Here's the lowdown on how to use cups to measure.

For flours, starches, and powdered sugar:

1. If it isn't already, transfer your flour, starch, or powdered sugar from the bag to a storage container large enough to hold it.

2. Stir with a fork to lighten it.

3. Spoon into the appropriate dry-cup measure. (If the recipe calls for 1 cup flour, you want to use a measuring cup that holds exactly 1 cup.)

4. Level the ingredient with a straight-edge tool like a metal icing spatula, the back of a knife, or a chopstick. (If you level the measuring cup over a piece of parchment paper, you can return the excess to its storage container.)

For Coconut Sugar, Evaporated Cane Juice, and Granulated Maple Sugar:

1. Scoop the sugar into the measuring cup. Overfill the cup.

2. Level the sugar with a straight-edge tool like a metal icing spatula, the back of a knife, or a chopstick.

For Softened Coconut Oil, Butter, Lard, or Palm Shortening:

1. Scoop the softened fat from container to the appropriate measuring cup. Use the back of a spoon to press the fat into the cup. This gets rid of air pockets.

2. **Level it with a straight-edge tool like a metal icing spatula or the back of a knife.**

Measuring Spoons

Most kitchen scales aren't sensitive enough to weigh very small amounts of ingredients, like ¼ teaspoon salt or ½ teaspoon ground cinnamon. Look for metal nested measuring spoons; they tend to be more accurate than plastic or one-piece "slide" measuring spoons.

Scoops

Cookie Scoop

Want a pan of evenly baked, perfectly shaped cookies? Use a small scoop to drop the dough onto the pan. Look for one that measures 2 teaspoons to 1 tablespoon.

Muffin Scoop (Medium Ice Cream Scoop)

A muffin scoop makes it easy to fill muffin cups with the same amount of batter. Look for one that holds about ¼ cup. I suggest buying scoops at a restaurant supply store. Commercial scoops will be labeled "#16" (this means there are 16 scoops in a quart).

Spatulas

Metal Icing Spatula

I use an 8-inch-long metal spatula, either straight or angled, to evenly spread thick batters in pans. The straight ones are great for spreading frosting on cakes and cupcakes.

Rubber or Silicone Spatula

Get every last drop of batter out of your mixing bowls with this handy tool. I like one-piece silicone spatulas—they are heatproof and easy to clean. I prefer flat ones to "spoonulas" that look kind of like, well, spoons. The flat ones make it easier to neatly scrape out bowls.

Wooden Spoons

Many of the recipes in this book use wooden spoons. Choose sturdy ones that are about 12 inches long.

Baking Pans

Cake Pans

I prefer straight-sided pans. They don't neatly nest inside each other, but I find that cakes bake more evenly in them than they do in pans with flared sides.

For the recipes in this book, you'll need the following cake pans:
8 x 2-inch round
8 x 8 x 2-inch square
9 x 9 x 2-inch square

Doughnut Pans

This book contains several recipes for baked doughnuts. Pick up a doughnut pan or two from a kitchen supply store. They're totally worth the cost.

Muffin Pans

You want a standard-size muffin pan, not Texas or jumbo. This is what you'll use for cupcakes, too. There's also one recipe in the book that uses a mini muffin pan.

Pie Pans

Use a standard 9-inch pie plate, not a deep-dish one. Grain-free crust tends to break apart as you try to fit it into the pan and doesn't take kindly to being baked in a deep pan.

Rimmed Baking Sheet

Also called a "half-sheet pan" (about 18 by 13 inches). This is the best pan for baking cookies. If space allows, keep a few of these on hand. That way, when you bake cookies, you won't need to wait for the pan to cool before starting the next batch.

Cookware

Cast-Iron Skillet

Look for an 8-inch cast-iron skillet. You can purchase it pre-seasoned, which is easiest, or season it yourself according to the instructions that come with it. Keep your cast-iron pan well seasoned by drying it immediately after you wash it and wiping it with a thin layer of neutral liquid oil, like grapeseed oil.

Griddle

A griddle is a large, flat cooking surface that fits over one or two burners on the stovetop. It can be seasoned cast iron or heavy aluminum with a nonstick coating. Use a nonstick griddle for pancakes or making naan (page 73).

Nonstick Frying Pan

A nonstick 8-inch pan makes it easy to make crepes, sandwich wraps, and tortillas. If you don't

cook in nonstick cookware, be sure to use a very well seasoned cast iron pan or the batters will stick.

Other Tools You Need

Kitchen Scale

Throughout the book, you'll find the ingredients listed in grams (weight) and cups (volume). But I really, really, really want you to use gram measurements. So yes, you need a kitchen scale. Grain-free flours vary from manufacturer to manufacturer, and bakers tend to measure "cups" of flour differently. One baker might fill a measuring cup with four ounces of flour while another might pack it with six ounces. Those extra two ounces can throw a recipe off—especially if it's coconut flour. I've also given weight measurements for liquid ingredients such as oils, maple syrup, honey, and eggs.

For the best results, please (please, please, please) use a kitchen scale. You want one that measures in single grams; it should not round up to the nearest 5 grams.

BAKER'S NOTE: *How to Use a Kitchen Scale*

1. **Place the mixing bowl (for dry ingredients) or liquid measuring cup (for liquids) on the scale.**
2. **Press the zero button (also called the "tare" button). The scale should now read zero (0).**
3. **Pour the ingredient into the container to the needed weight.**
4. **Hit the zero button to clear the scale before adding the next ingredient.**
5. **Repeat until all ingredients are measured.**

Electric Mixer (Handheld or Stand)

Most of the recipes in this book are too small to warrant using a stand mixer. Handheld mixers zip through thick grain-free batters. I love my KitchenAid handheld.

If you want to use a stand mixer, use the flat paddle attachment to mix batters. I suggest a KitchenAid with a 4.5 quart bowl.

Mixing Bowls

Ideally, you want at least one small, one medium, and one large mixing bowl in the kitchen.

Paper Cupcake Liners

Grain-free cupcakes and muffins tend to stick to the pan. Paper liners solve this problem. Look for ones made of greaseproof paper.

Parchment Paper

It's a good idea to keep both parchment paper sheets and precut rounds on hand. Slip parchment sheets into rimmed baking sheets when you make cookies and use the rounds in cake pans. Grain-free cakes, especially ones made with coconut flour, love to stick even if you grease the pan.

Thermometers

Instant-Read Thermometer

Temperature matters, especially when working with yeast. Using an instant-read thermometer ensures that your water is at the correct temperature to make yeast happy and can also tell you if the interior of your bread has baked enough.

Oven Thermometer

Most oven temperatures do not match the setting. Place an oven thermometer in your oven and adjust the temperature setting as needed.

Waffle Iron

A traditional waffle iron or one that makes thick Belgium waffles, the choice is yours.

Wire Cooling Racks

Look for wire racks with a tight grid pattern and small feet. Cooling baked goods on a wire rack allows steam to escape, thereby preventing sogginess.

Nice to Have But Not 100% Necessary

Food Processor

For mixing cookie dough and making nut butters.

High-Powered Blender

For making nut butters.

Pastry Cutter

For cutting fat into flour when making doughs.

Pizza Wheel

For scoring crackers and cutting pasta dough.

Breakfast

Lazy Morning Waffles

Big, Fluffy Pancakes

Silver Dollar Pancakes

Marble Pancakes

Gingerbread Pancakes

French-Style Crepes

Old-Fashion' Cake Doughnuts

Vermont Maple Doughnuts

Lemon-Glazed Chocolate Doughnuts

Cinnamon Streusel Coffee Cake

"Buttermilk" Biscuits

Pumpkin Spice Muffins

Garam Masala Pumpkin Muffins

Banana-Date Muffins

Zippy Lemon Poppy Seed Muffins

Cinnamon Streusel
Coffee Cake, page 50

Lazy Morning Waffles

coconut-free if made with butter

Light and crispy, these waffles make a lazy weekend morning even better. Serve them with a drizzle of maple syrup or top with something savory, like an egg or slices of ham.

Active Time: 10 minutes
Cook Time: varies depending on the waffle iron
Yield: about 4 Belgian waffles or 6 regular waffles, depending on the size of the iron

142 grams (1 ¼ cups) finely ground almond flour

57 grams (½ cup) tapioca starch

2 teaspoons baking powder, homemade (page 210) or grain-free store-bought

½ teaspoon salt

113 grams (½ cup) milk, dairy-free or traditional

1 large egg (about 50 grams out of the shell)

28 grams (2 tablespoons) coconut oil or unsalted butter, melted and cooled slightly

1 teaspoon vanilla extract

Roasted Almond Butter (page 201) or Coconut Butter (page 204), for serving

Preheat the waffle iron.

Whisk the almond flour, tapioca starch, baking powder, and salt together in a medium mixing bowl. Add the milk, egg, melted coconut oil, and vanilla and whisk until smooth.

Lightly grease the waffle iron with nonstick cooking spray or brush with melted coconut oil. Pour batter into the iron as directed by the manufacturer. Cook until the waffle is brown and crisp. Repeat with the remaining batter. Enjoy right away, topped with almond or coconut butter.

· ·

Leftover waffles freeze well. Allow the waffles to cool. Stack them with pieces of parchment or waxed paper in between. Slide the stack into a freezer bag, seal, and freeze for up to 6 weeks. When you are in the mood for a waffle, thaw in 30-second intervals in the microwave until warm.

· ·

Big, Fluffy Pancakes `coconut-free`

These pancakes take only minutes to make but taste like you spent lots of time on them—which is great when you're still bleary-eyed from sleep.

Active Time: 10 minutes
Cook Time: 5 minutes per batch
Yield: 12 (4-inch) pancakes

142 grams (1 ¼ cups) finely ground almond flour

57 grams (½ cup) tapioca starch*

1 ½ teaspoons baking powder, homemade (page 210) or grain-free store-bought

½ teaspoon salt

3 large eggs (about 150 grams out of the shell)

2 tablespoons dark maple syrup (optional)

2 to 3 tablespoons milk, dairy-free or traditional

1 teaspoon vanilla extract

* For starch-free pancakes, omit the tapioca starch and increase the almond flour to 170 grams (1 ½ cups). The pancakes will be slightly denser but still delicious!

Whisk the almond flour, tapioca starch, baking powder, and salt together in a medium mixing bowl. Add the eggs, maple syrup, 2 tablespoons milk, and the vanilla and stir with a wooden spoon until a batter forms. It should resemble thick cake batter. If batter is too thick to drop on the griddle, add one additional tablespoon of milk.

Heat a griddle over medium-high heat. Lightly grease it with nonstick cooking spray or brush with melted coconut oil.

Spoon about 3 tablespoons batter per pancake onto the griddle. Cook until bubbles appear at the edges of the pancake, about three minutes. Flip and cook for an additional minute or two, until lightly brown. Repeat with remaining batter. Enjoy right away.

· ·

Leftover pancakes freeze well. Allow the pancakes to cool. Stack them with pieces of parchment or waxed paper in between. Slide the stack into a freezer bag, seal, and freeze for up to 6 weeks. When you are in the mood for pancakes, thaw in 30-second intervals in the microwave until warm.

· ·

Variations

Blueberry-Lemon Pancakes: Stir the grated zest of 1 lemon and ¾ cup washed and drained blueberries into the batter just before cooking.

Chocolate Chip Pancakes: Replace the maple syrup with 2 tablespoons coconut sugar or evaporated cane juice. Sprinkle about 2 teaspoons mini dairy-free dark chocolate chips on each pancake as soon as you spoon the batter onto the pan.

Silver Dollar Pancakes `almond-free`

Making coconut flour pancakes turned out to be, as my husband would say, "a dilly of a pickle," or as I would say, "a pain in the . . . " My first attempts would not flip. At all. The moisture-loving coconut flour kept the batter wet and the pancakes didn't form enough of a crust to flip. After lots of testing, I finally created a recipe I love that is flippable. The pancakes are satisfyingly eggy; they're also sugar- and nut-free.

One word of caution: going larger than 1 tablespoon of batter per pancake makes these a little hard to flip. Make 'em small and eat a big stack!

Active Time: 5 minutes
Cook Time: 5 minutes per batch
Yield: about 16 pancakes

36 grams (⅓ cup) coconut flour

¼ teaspoon baking powder, homemade (page 210) or grain-free store-bought

¼ teaspoon salt

4 large eggs (about 200 grams out of the shell)

57 to 85 grams (4 to 6 tablespoons) milk, dairy-free or traditional

1 tablespoon coconut oil or unsalted butter, melted and cooled slightly

1 teaspoon vanilla extract

Whisk the coconut flour, baking powder, and salt together in a medium mixing bowl. Add the eggs, 4 tablespoons milk, coconut oil, and vanilla and whisk until smooth. If batter is too thick to drop from a spoon, stir in the additional 2 tablespoons milk.

Heat a griddle over medium-high heat. Lightly grease it with melted coconut oil or nonstick cooking spray.

Drop 1 tablespoon batter per pancake onto the griddle with a spoon. Use the back of the spoon to spread the batter out a little. Cook until bubbles appear on the surface of the pancake and edges are set, about 3 minutes. Flip and cook an additional minute, until golden brown. Repeat with the remaining batter.

Serve warm with syrup or fresh fruit, if desired.

. . . .
These pancakes are best enjoyed as soon as they are made.
. . . .

Marble Pancakes `coconut-free`

Move over, chocolate chip pancakes! This breakfast treat, inspired by marble birthday cake, is edging in on your turf.

You'll need a small plastic squeeze bottle for this recipe, which you can pick up at any local kitchen or cake decorating supply store.

Active Time: about 15 minutes
Cook Time: 5 minutes per batch
Yield: 12 (4-inch) pancakes

142 grams (1 ¼ cups) finely ground almond flour

57 grams (½ cup) tapioca starch

1 ½ teaspoons baking powder, homemade (page 210) or grain-free store-bought

¼ teaspoon salt

3 large eggs (about 150 grams out of the shell)

3 tablespoons milk, dairy-free or traditional

2 tablespoons dark maple syrup

1 tablespoon cocoa powder, natural or Dutch-process

1 teaspoon vanilla extract

Whisk the almond flour, tapioca starch, baking powder, and salt together in a medium mixing bowl. Add the eggs, 2 tablespoons of the milk, and the maple syrup and whisk until smooth.

Pour about ½ cup of the batter into a small mixing bowl. Stir in the cocoa powder and the remaining 1 tablespoon milk until smooth. Pour the chocolate batter into a small squeeze bottle with a wide tip opening.

Whisk the vanilla into the remaining batter.

Heat a nonstick griddle over medium-high heat. Lightly grease it with nonstick cooking spray or brush lightly with melted coconut oil.

Spoon about 3 tablespoons of the vanilla batter per pancake onto the griddle. You want the batter to sizzle as it hits the griddle. Using the squeeze bottle, drizzle some chocolate batter on each pancake. Make whatever type of design you want—a swirl, polka dots, a smiley face, or hearts are fun to do. Cook the pancakes until the edges are set, about 3 minutes. Flip and cook an additional minute or so, until lightly golden brown. Repeat with the remaining batter.* Enjoy right away.

• •
Leftover pancakes freeze well. Allow the pancakes to cool. Stack them with pieces of parchment or waxed paper in between. Slide the stack into a freezer bag, seal, and freeze for up to 6 weeks. When you are in the mood for pancakes, thaw in 30–second intervals in the microwave until warm.
• •

* At the end, you might have a little chocolate batter leftover. I cook this up and call the chocolate pancake a cook's treat!

Gingerbread Pancakes `almond-free`

Why confine gingerbread to the holiday season? That's just silly! I make these pancakes all year long. In the summer, try them topped with slices of ripe strawberries or peaches. The fruit and ginger complement each other really well.

Active Time: 10 minutes
Cook Time: 5 minutes per batch
Yield: 12 pancakes

36 grams (⅓ cup) coconut flour

2 teaspoons ground ginger

1 teaspoon ground cinnamon

½ teaspoon baking powder, homemade (page 210) or grain-free store-bought

½ teaspoon salt

4 large eggs (about 200 grams out of the shell)

3 tablespoons milk, dairy-free or traditional, plus more as needed

2 tablespoons unsulphured molasses or dark maple syrup

1 tablespoon coconut oil or unsalted butter, melted and cooled slightly

1 teaspoon vanilla extract

Whisk the coconut flour, ginger, cinnamon, baking powder, and salt together in a medium mixing bowl. Whisk in the eggs, milk, molasses, melted coconut oil, and vanilla until smooth. If batter is too thick to drop from a spoon, stir in additional milk (start with one tablespoon and go from there).

Heat a nonstick griddle over medium-high heat. Lightly grease it with nonstick cooking spray or brush lightly with melted coconut oil.

Spoon about 3 tablespoons batter per pancake onto the griddle. As you spoon the batter, spread it out just a little with the back of a spoon or ladle. Cook until bubbles appear on the surface of the pancake and the edges are set, about 3 minutes. Flip and cook an additional minute or so, until golden brown. Repeat with remaining batter. Serve warm.

· ·
These pancakes are best enjoyed as soon as they are cooked.
· ·

French-Style Crepes

Think of these crepes as a blank canvas. Spread them with homemade Almond-Ella (page 202) or your favorite nut butter. Even simpler, throw some fresh berries on a warm crepe, roll it up, and call it delicious.

Active Time: 20 minutes
Cook Time: about 4 minutes per crepe
Yield: 6 crepes

36 grams (⅓ cup) coconut flour

2 tablespoons tapioca starch

¼ teaspoon salt

3 large eggs (about 150 grams out of the shell)

113 grams (½ cup) milk, dairy-free or traditional, plus more as needed (see Baker's Note)

1 tablespoon honey

1 teaspoon vanilla extract

BAKER'S NOTE: *Crepe Batter Consistency*

The consistency of the crepe batter is key to making a perfect batch. You want it thin and pourable. Since this batter contains coconut flour, it tends to thicken as it sits. You might need to adjust the consistency as you go along. Before you make each crepe, lift some of the batter with a spoon and pour it back into the bowl. It should flow. If it drops in clumps, add a splash of milk (about 1 tablespoon) until it is fluid.

Whisk the coconut flour, tapioca starch, and salt together in a medium mixing bowl. Add the eggs, milk, honey, and vanilla and whisk until smooth. Allow the batter to rest for 5 minutes.

Spray an 8-inch nonstick frying pan lightly with nonstick cooking spray or brush about ½ teaspoon melted coconut oil on the pan. Heat the pan over medium heat until hot but not smoking.

Pour ¼ cup batter into the pan. Immediately and quickly, rotate the pan to spread the batter out to cover the bottom.

Place the pan back on the burner. Cook until the batter is set, about 2 minutes. The surface will look flat. Run a rubber spatula all around the edge of the crepe. Flip the crepe and cook another minute or so, until golden brown. Remove the crepe and place it on a plate. Cover the plate with a dry towel to keep the crepes warm. Repeat with remaining batter, greasing the pan and adjusting the consistency of the batter as needed. Serve warm or cool.

Store wrapped leftovers in the refrigerator and warm on low in the microwave for 20 seconds.

Old-Fashion' Cake Doughnuts `almond-free`

My grandparents drank coffee each morning at a little bakery in Burlington, Vermont. They called it "The Bakery" and to this day I don't know what the place was actually called. Along with their morning cups of coffee and conversations with the locals, they ate old-fashioned cake doughnuts—or, as the sign proclaimed, "donuts." Those simple treats inspired this recipe. A whisper of nutmeg gives it that perfect bakery-style flavor.

Active Time: 10 minutes
Bake Time: 15 minutes per pan
Yield: 12 doughnuts

100 grams (⅔ cup) coconut sugar or evaporated cane juice

57 grams (½ cup) coconut flour

57 grams (½ cup) tapioca starch

1 teaspoon baking powder, homemade (page 210) or grain-free store-bought

1 teaspoon ground nutmeg

¾ teaspoon salt

57 grams (¼ cup) coconut oil or unsalted butter, melted and cooled slightly

2 large eggs (about 100 grams out of the shell)

170 grams (¾ cup) milk, dairy-free or traditional

1 teaspoon vanilla extract

Adjust an oven rack to the middle position and preheat the oven to 350°F. Grease two 6-cavity doughnut pans* with nonstick cooking spray, melted coconut oil, or melted butter.

Whisk the coconut sugar, coconut flour, tapioca starch, baking powder, nutmeg, and salt together in a medium mixing bowl. Add the melted coconut oil, eggs, milk, and vanilla and whisk until smooth. The batter will be thick.

Spoon the batter into the prepared pans, filling the cavities about three-quarters full. (If you have a piping bag and large plain pastry tip kicking around the kitchen, use those instead.) Lightly tap the pans on the counter to settle the batter.

Bake the doughnuts until they are golden brown and spring back to the touch, about 15 minutes.

Allow the doughnuts to cool in the pans on a wire rack for 5 minutes, then turn them out onto the rack to cool completely.

. . . .

Doughnuts are best enjoyed the day they are baked. Freeze leftovers, wrapped in plastic wrap and placed in a freezer container, for up to 1 month.

. . . .

* If you own only one doughnut pan, no problem! Bake six doughnuts. Allow them to cool in the pan as directed, then turn them out onto the rack. Wipe out the pan and grease it again. Repeat using the remaining batter.

Vermont Maple Doughnuts

A doughnut that tastes like a syrup-drenched pancake? It doesn't get more breakfast than that!

Active Time: 10 minutes
Bake Time: 15 minutes per pan
Yield: 12 doughnuts

170 grams (1 ½ cups) finely ground almond flour

1 ½ teaspoons baking powder, homemade (page 210) or grain-free store-bought

¾ teaspoon salt

½ teaspoon ground cinnamon

½ teaspoon ground nutmeg

2 large eggs (about 100 grams out of the shell)

100 grams (⅓ cup) dark maple syrup

1 teaspoon vanilla extract

Adjust an oven rack to the middle position and preheat the oven to 350°F. Grease two 6-cavity doughnut pans* with nonstick cooking spray or brush with melted coconut oil.

Whisk the almond flour, baking powder, salt, cinnamon, and nutmeg together in a large mixing bowl. Add the eggs, maple syrup, and vanilla and stir to combine. You can use a wooden spoon or hand-held mixer.

Spoon the batter into the prepared pans, filling each cavity about one-half full. (You can also use a piping bag and large plain pastry tip.) Lightly tap the pans on the counter to settle the batter.

Bake the doughnuts until they are golden brown and spring back to the touch, about 15 minutes.

Allow the doughnuts to cool in the pans on a wire rack for 5 minutes, then turn them out onto the rack to cool completely.

. . . .
Doughnuts are best enjoyed the day they are baked. Freeze cooled leftovers in a freezer bag for up to 1 month.
. . . .

* If you only own one doughnut pan, no problem! Bake six doughnuts. Allow them to cool in the pan as directed, then turn them out onto the rack. Wipe out the pan and grease it again. Repeat using the remaining batter.

Lemon-Glazed Chocolate Doughnuts almond-free

My favorite doughnut? Whichever kind I happen to be eating, of course! But seriously, chocolate doughnuts are a favorite-favorite. I love them iced with a lemon glaze, but if you want to keep the sugar down, feel free to skip it.

Active Time: 10 minutes
Bake Time: about 12 minutes per pan
Yield: 12 doughnuts

Doughnuts

36 grams (⅓ cup) coconut flour

25 grams (¼ cup) Dutch-process cocoa powder*

1 teaspoon baking powder, homemade (page 210) or grain-free store-bought

¼ teaspoon ground nutmeg

¼ teaspoon salt

113 grams (⅓ cup) honey

57 grams (¼ cup) coconut oil, melted and cooled slightly

4 large eggs (about 200 grams out of the shell)

Lemon Glaze**

57 grams (½ cup) powdered sugar, homemade (page 210) or grain-free store-bought

2 teaspoons freshly squeezed lemon juice

* If you only have natural cocoa powder on hand, use it and replace the baking powder with ½ teaspoon baking soda.

** If you don't like lemon, replace the lemon juice with 1 teaspoon dairy-free or traditional milk and 1 teaspoon vanilla extract.

Adjust an oven rack to the middle position and preheat the oven to 350°F. Grease two 6-cavity doughnut pans* with nonstick cooking spray or brush with melted coconut oil.

Whisk the coconut flour, cocoa powder, baking powder, nutmeg, and salt together in a medium mixing bowl. Add honey and melted coconut oil and whisk until smooth. Add the eggs and mix well.

Spoon the batter into the prepared pans, filling each cavity about half full. (You can also use a piping bag and large pastry tip.) Lightly tap the pans on the counter to settle the batter.

Bake until the doughnuts are puffy and a toothpick inserted into the center of one of them comes out clean, about 12 minutes.

Allow the doughnuts to cool in the pans on a wire rack for 5 minutes, then turn them out onto the rack to cool completely.

When the doughnuts are cool, make the glaze: Stir the powdered sugar and lemon juice together in a small mixing bowl. The glaze should be thick but pourable. If it's too thick, add a little extra lemon juice. Place a piece of parchment under the wire rack. Dip the tops of the doughnuts, one at a time, in the glaze, then set on the wire rack. The glaze will drip down the sides. Allow the glaze to set for about ten minutes before serving.

. . . .

Doughnuts are best enjoyed the day they are baked. Wrap leftover doughnuts with plastic wrap and store at room temperature.

. . . .

* If you only own one doughnut pan, no problem! Bake six doughnuts. Allow them to cool in the pan as directed, then turn them out onto the rack. Wipe out the pan and grease it again. Repeat using the remaining batter.

Cinnamon Streusel Coffee Cake

My love of coffee cake started years before I tasted a sip of coffee. My mom made it often during my childhood, always as an after-dinner treat. This recipe, with its sweet cinnamon flavor, makes a nice breakfast or dessert—coffee optional!

Active Time: 15 minutes
Bake Time: about 30 minutes
Yield: 1 (8-inch round) cake

Cake

198 grams (1 ¾ cups) finely ground almond flour

21 grams (3 tablespoons) coconut flour

1 ½ teaspoons baking powder, homemade (page 210) or grain-free store-bought

½ teaspoon salt

57 grams (¼ cup) coconut oil, solid, or unsalted butter, softened

4 large eggs (about 200 grams out of the shell)

100 grams (⅓ cup) dark maple syrup

1 teaspoon vanilla extract

Streusel

2 tablespoons granulated maple sugar

1 ½ teaspoons ground cinnamon

Adjust an oven rack to the middle position and preheat the oven to 350°F. Grease an 8-inch round cake pan with nonstick cooking spray or brush lightly with melted coconut oil. Place an 8-inch round of parchment paper in the bottom of the pan.

Whisk the almond flour, coconut flour, baking powder, and salt together in a medium mixing bowl. Use a pastry cutter or your fingers to cut the coconut oil into the dry ingredients until the mixture resembles a coarse meal. You don't want any large nubs of coconut oil. If you use your fingers, work in the coconut oil with a quick snapping motion. Remove 2 tablespoons of the dry mixture for the streusel, place in a small mixing bowl, and set aside.

Whisk the eggs, one at a time, into the remaining dry ingredients. Allow each egg to be incorporated before you add the next. After you add the final egg, whisk in the maple syrup and vanilla. Spread the batter into the prepared pan.

Prepare the streusel: stir the maple sugar and cinnamon into the reserved flour mixture. Sprinkle it evenly over the batter.

Bake until a cake tester inserted in the center of the cake comes out clean, about 30 minutes.

Place the pan on a wire rack and allow the cake to cool completely in the pan.

· ·
Store on the counter, covered tightly, for up to 3 days.
· ·

"Buttermilk" Biscuits

egg-free; coconut-free if made with buttermilk

A basket of these biscuits is the perfect side to a roast chicken. They are also great for breakfast egg sandwiches. Unlike classic cut-out biscuits, you form these by gently rolling the dough between your palms. If the dough sticks to your hands (more common in summer when it's humid than in winter), dust your palms with tapioca starch.

Active Time: 15 minutes
Bake Time: about 20 minutes
Yield: 8 biscuits

227 grams (2 cups) finely ground almond flour

28 grams (¼ cup) tapioca starch

2 teaspoons baking powder, homemade (page 210) or grain-free store-bought

½ teaspoon salt

57 grams (¼ cup) full-fat coconut milk or traditional buttermilk

1 tablespoon white vinegar (omit if using buttermilk)

Preheat the oven to 425°F. Line a rimmed baking sheet with parchment paper.

Whisk the almond flour, tapioca starch, baking powder, and salt together in a medium mixing bowl. Stir in coconut milk and vinegar with a wooden spoon.

Gently roll dough, about ¼ cup for each biscuit, between your palms and place on the prepared baking sheet, spaced about 2 inches apart.

Bake until edges are golden brown, about 20 minutes.

Remove from the oven and allow the biscuits to cool on the baking sheet for 5 minutes.

. . . .
Biscuits are best enjoyed the day they are baked. Freeze cooled leftovers, wrapped in plastic wrap and placed in a freezer container, for up to 2 weeks.
. . . .

BAKER'S NOTE: *Breakfast Sandwich Biscuits*

Want a soft and tender biscuit for breakfast sandwiches? Here's how to easily modify the recipe: increase the coconut milk to 113 grams (½ cup). The batter will be thin. Drop the batter, about ¼ cup each, using a muffin scoop, onto the prepared baking sheet. Bake as directed.

Pumpkin Spice Muffins `almond-free`

The pumpkin spice craze would irritate me if pumpkin spice wasn't so darn tasty. Most of the grumbling centers around the fact that most items—from lattes to chocolate—don't contain any pumpkin. These muffins, smarty pants that they are, skirt the brouhaha by containing both pumpkin spice and pumpkin. Win-win!

Active Time: 10 minutes
Bake Time: about 30 minutes
Yield: 8 muffins

36 grams (⅓ cup) coconut flour

2 teaspoons pumpkin pie spice, homemade (recipe follows) or store-bought

½ teaspoon baking powder, homemade (page 210) or grain-free store-bought

¼ teaspoon salt

4 large eggs (about 200 grams out of the shell)

170 grams (¾ cup) pure pumpkin puree (see Baker's Note, page 177)

100 grams (⅓ cup) dark maple syrup

28 grams (2 tablespoons) coconut oil or unsalted butter, melted and cooled slightly

Adjust an oven rack to the middle position and preheat the oven to 350°F. Line eight standard-size muffin cups with paper liners.

Whisk the coconut flour, pumpkin pie spice, baking powder, and salt together in a large mixing bowl. Add the eggs, pumpkin puree, maple syrup, and melted coconut oil and whisk until smooth. Scoop the batter into the prepared muffin cups, filling each cup about three-quarters full.

Bake until the muffins are set, golden brown, and spring back to the touch, about 30 minutes.

Transfer the muffins to a wire rack to cool completely.

Wrap cooled muffins tightly and store on the counter for up to 3 days. Freeze, wrapped in plastic wrap and placed in a freezer container, for up to 1 month.

Pumpkin Pie Spice

If you don't have pumpkin pie spice on hand, you can make your own! You'll have a little bit leftover from this recipe. Go ahead and sprinkle it in coffee or homemade hot chocolate.

Yield: about 1 tablespoon

2 teaspoons ground cinnamon

1 teaspoon ground ginger

½ teaspoon ground cloves

¼ teaspoon ground nutmeg

Stir the spices together in a small mixing bowl.

Garam Masala Pumpkin Muffins `coconut-free`

Garam masala, an Indian spice blend that's traditionally used in savory dishes, brings a spicy warmth to these muffins. In fact, garam masala translates to "warm spice mix." In India, the ingredients differ depending on the region and the cook. It usually contains cinnamon, nutmeg, cloves, cardamom, mace, peppercorns, coriander, and cumin. I buy mine from Penzeys (see Sources, page 211) but use whatever blend you love.

Active Time: 10 minutes
Bake Time: about 30 minutes
Yield: 12 muffins

142 grams (1 ¼ cups) finely ground almond flour

28 grams (¼ cup) tapioca starch

2 teaspoons garam masala*

1 ½ teaspoons baking powder, homemade (page 210) or grain-free store-bought

½ teaspoon salt

300 grams (1 ¼ cups) pure pumpkin puree (see Baker's Note, page 177)

3 large eggs (about 150 grams out of the shell)

100 grams (⅓ cup) dark maple syrup

* If you don't have (or love) garam masala, replace it with an equal amount of pumpkin pie spice (homemade, page 54, or store-bought).

Adjust an oven rack to the middle position and preheat the oven to 350°F. Line 12 standard-size muffin cups with paper liners.

Whisk the almond flour, tapioca starch, garam masala, baking powder, and salt together in a medium mixing bowl. Add the pumpkin puree, eggs, and maple syrup and whisk until smooth.

Scoop the batter into the prepared muffin cups, filling each cup about three-quarters full.

Bake until the muffins are set, golden brown, and spring back to the touch, about 30 minutes.

Transfer the muffins to a wire rack to cool completely.

. . . .

Wrap cooled muffins and store on the counter for up to 3 days. Freeze, wrapped in plastic wrap and placed in a freezer container, for up to 1 month.

. . . .

Banana-Date Muffins `almond-free`

I like my banana bread plain—no cinnamon or raisins for me, thank you. I also kinda-sorta dislike change. So when a friend made a batch of gluten-free banana-date bread, I knew I wouldn't like it. I'm open minded like that (ahem). Only I did like it! I liked it a lot. Maybe I need to give this whole "try new things" a try. . .

Active Time: 20 minutes
Bake Time: about 35 minutes
Yield: 9 muffins

10 pitted dates (about 70 grams), chopped into bite-size pieces*

1 large banana, peeled and mashed (about 125 grams / ½ cup)

36 grams (⅓ cup) coconut flour

1 teaspoon ground cinnamon

1 teaspoon baking powder, homemade (page 210) or grain-free store-bought

½ teaspoon salt

3 large eggs (about 150 grams out of the shell)

75 grams (¼ cup) dark maple syrup

* I prefer to chop whole dates for this recipe. You can use store-bought chopped dates if you'd like; you'll need about ½ cup.

Adjust an oven rack to the middle position and preheat the oven to 350°F. Line 9 standard-size muffin cups with paper liners.

Place the dates in a 2-cup liquid measuring cup. Cover the dates with hot water, and allow to soak for 10 minutes.

While the dates soak, peel the banana and mash it with a fork in a small mixing bowl. It's okay if small pieces of banana remain.

Whisk the coconut flour, cinnamon, baking powder, and salt together in a medium mixing bowl. Add the eggs and maple syrup and whisk until smooth. The batter will be thick.

Drain and discard the water from the dates. Switch to a wooden spoon and stir the dates and mashed banana into the batter. Scoop the batter into the prepared muffin cups, filling each cup about three-quarters full.

Bake until the muffins are set and golden brown, about 35 minutes.

Transfer the muffins to a wire rack to cool completely.

Wrap the cooled muffins with plastic wrap and store on the counter for up to 3 days, or freeze for up to 1 month.

Zippy Lemon Poppy Seed Muffins

starch-free

Lemon zest and juice add a nice citrus kick to these muffins.

Active Time: 15 minutes
Bake Time: 25 minutes
Yield: 12 muffins

142 grams (1 ¼ cups) finely ground almond flour

57 grams (⅓ cup) coconut sugar or evaporated cane juice

14 grams (2 tablespoons) coconut flour

1 tablespoon poppy seeds

1 teaspoon baking soda

¼ teaspoon salt

3 large eggs (about 150 grams out of the shell)

2 tablespoons almond oil, or coconut oil or unsalted butter, melted and cooled slightly

Finely grated zest of 1 lemon (about 1 tablespoon)*

3 tablespoons freshly squeezed lemon juice

1 teaspoon vanilla extract

* Remember to zest the lemon before you juice it!

Adjust an oven rack to the middle position and preheat the oven to 350°F. Line 12 standard-size muffin cups with paper liners.

Whisk together almond flour, coconut sugar, coconut flour, poppy seeds, baking soda, and salt in a large mixing bowl. Add the eggs, almond oil, lemon zest, lemon juice, and vanilla and stir with a wooden spoon until the batter is smooth. Scoop the batter into the prepared muffin cups, filling each cup about two-thirds full.

Bake until golden brown and a cake tester inserted in the center of a muffin comes out clean, about 25 minutes. Let cool for 10 minutes before serving.

Wrap cooled muffins and store on the counter for up to 3 days. Freeze, wrapped in plastic wrap and placed in a freezer container, for up to 1 month.

On the Savory Side

"Lean Dough" for Baguettes, Hard Rolls, and Bagels

Classic Focaccia

Naan

Quick Pizza Crust

Fresh Pasta Dough

Savory Dinner Muffins

Garlic, Onion, and Herb Waffles

Hogs in a Sweater

Not-So-Common Crackers

Flour Tortillas

Sandwich Wraps

Classic Focaccia, page 70

"Lean Dough" for Baguettes, Hard Rolls, and Bagels `coconut-free`

One dough to rule them all! That's how the Lord of the Rings quote went, right?

This almond-flour dough makes fabulous crusty baguettes, hard rolls, and chewy New York–style bagels. It's based on classic wheat-based "lean dough," so called because it contains little or no fat. While this recipe isn't fat-free, it works like a classic lean dough. So that's how I think of it!

Active Time: 15 minutes
Yield: 1 baguette or 6 hard rolls or 8 bagels

113 grams (½ cup) warm water (100° to 110°F)

1 packet (2 ½ teaspoons) active dry yeast*

227 grams (2 cups) finely ground almond flour

113 grams (1 cup) tapioca starch, plus more for dusting the counter

1 teaspoon baking powder, homemade (page 210) or grain-free store-bought

½ teaspoon salt

* You can also use instant yeast. Whisk it into the dry ingredients along with the salt. Then add 113 grams warm water (120° to 130°F) and stir with a wooden spoon until the dough holds together.

Stir the water and yeast together in a small mixing bowl until the yeast dissolves. Allow to stand for 5 minutes.

Whisk the almond flour, tapioca starch, baking powder, and salt together in a medium mixing bowl. Add the yeast mixture and stir with a wooden spoon until the dough holds together. Allow the dough to rest for 5 minutes.

Lightly dust the counter with tapioca starch. Turn the dough out onto the counter and knead it a few times, until smooth.

BAKER'S NOTE: *Troubleshooting Yeast Breads*

Here are some issues to keep in mind when baking grain-free yeast-raised breads.

The dough is dry.

This can happen. If your dough looks dry, turn it out onto your counter. Drizzle with 2 tablespoons water. Gather the dough together by squeezing it and begin to knead. The oils in the almond flour will release and a dough should form. If after a minute or two a dough hasn't formed, drizzle it with an additional tablespoon of water and knead until smooth.

The dough is hard to roll.

If your dough crumbles, knead it until smooth. If it's still dry, knead in an additional tablespoon of water, then reroll.

The dough is too wet.

Add an additional tablespoon or two of tapioca starch.

The dough didn't rise.

This dough does not rise as high as traditional gluten-based or gluten-free dough. If it doesn't rise at all, it might be a yeast issue. See page 22 for how to work with yeast.

The bread staled quickly.

Like most grain-free baked goods, breads stale rather quickly. They are best enjoyed the day they are baked.

Baguette

Active Time: 20 minutes, plus 1 hour for rising
Bake Time: 20 minutes
Yield: 1 baguette

1 recipe Lean Dough (page 65)

Roll the dough into a 12-inch-long log.

Line a baguette pan or rimmed baking sheet with a piece of parchment paper. (I like to bake baguettes in a baguette pan. It helps the bread hold its shape.) Place the baguette in the prepared pan. Cover with a piece of plastic wrap and a dry kitchen towel. Allow the dough to rise in a warm place for 1 hour. The dough won't double in size but you will see it lift slightly.

Preheat the oven to 425°F.

Use a sharp knife to make three diagonal cuts across the top of the baguette. Spray the loaf lightly with water. If you don't have a spray bottle, brush a little water on the baguette with a pastry brush.

Bake until golden brown, about 20 minutes. Pierce the center of the baguette with an instant-read thermometer to determine if the loaf has baked all the way through. The internal temperature of the dough should reach 205°F. If the crust gets too dark before the loaf reaches the correct temperature, cover the loaf lightly with foil and continue to bake.

Allow the bread to cool on the pan for five minutes and then transfer to a wire rack to cool.

. . . .
The baguette is best enjoyed the day it's baked.
. . . .

Hard Rolls

Active Time: 15 minutes, plus 1 hour for rising
Bake Time: 15 minutes
Yield: 6 hard rolls

1 recipe Lean Dough (page 65)

Pat the dough into a circle and cut into six equal pieces. Round each piece into a ball, then gently flatten. You want the dough about 1-inch thick.

Line a rimmed baking sheet with parchment paper. Place the rolls on the baking sheet, cover with plastic wrap, and allow to rise in a warm place for 1 hour or until doubled in size.

Preheat the oven to 425°F.

Spray the rolls lightly with water. If you don't have a spray bottle, brush a little water on the rolls with a pastry brush.

Bake the rolls until golden brown, about 15 minutes.

Remove the rolls from oven and allow to cool on the pan. Enjoy warm or at room temperature.

. . . .
Hard rolls are best enjoyed the day they are baked.
. . . .

Bagels

Active Time: 60 minutes, plus 1 hour for rising
Bake Time: 15 minutes
Yield: 8 bagels

28 grams (¼ cup) tapioca starch, plus more for dusting the counter
1 recipe Lean Dough (page 65)

Line a rimmed baking sheet with parchment paper. Dust the counter lightly with additional tapioca starch.

Knead the measured tapioca starch into the dough.

Roll out the dough to a rectangle about ¾-inch thick. Cut the dough into rounds with a 2 ½-inch circle cutter. Cut a center hole from each round with 1-inch cutter. Reroll the dough scraps and cut more rounds, for a total of 8 bagels

Place the bagels on the prepared baking sheet, spaced 2 to 3 inches apart. Cover with plastic wrap and a dry kitchen towel. Allow the bagels to rise in a warm place for 1 hour, until the bagels almost double in size.

Preheat the oven to 425°F. Bring about 4 cups of water to a simmer in a small pot.

One at a time, slide a bagel into the simmering water. Simmer until it floats to the surface of the water, about 20 seconds. Remove with a slotted spoon and return bagel to the baking sheet. (If after 30 seconds it doesn't float, remove it from the water anyway.) Repeat with the remaining bagels.

Bake the bagels until golden brown, about 15 minutes. Allow them to cool on the pan for five minutes, then transfer to a wire rack to cool completely.

. . . .
Bagels are best enjoyed the day they are baked. Wrap leftover cooled bagels and freeze for up to 1 month.
. . . .

Variations

Sesame Seed Bagels: After you remove the bagels from the water, sprinkle them with 2 tablespoons sesame seeds.

Poppy Seed Bagels: After you remove the bagels from the water, sprinkle them with 2 tablespoons poppy seeds.

"Everything" Bagels: Whisk 1 tablespoon sesame seeds, 1 tablespoon poppy seeds, 1 teaspoon dried onion (not onion powder; see Sources, page 211), 1 teaspoon dried garlic (not garlic powder; see Sources, page 211), and 1 teaspoon kosher salt together in a small bowl. Sprinkle the bagels with this mixture after you remove them from the water.

Cinnamon Raisin Bagels: Knead 3 tablespoons raisins and 2 teaspoons ground cinnamon into the dough along with the tapioca starch. For sweet cinnamon-raisin bagels, also add 1 tablespoon granulated maple sugar.

Classic Focaccia coconut-free

Not only does this recipe make one heck of a chewy focaccia, it's also a bit of a science project. When you add the vinegar, you can see and hear the dough bubble as the baking soda and vinegar react. Yay, science!

Active Time: 10 minutes
Bake Time: about 20 minutes
Yield: 1 (8-inch) focaccia

227 grams (2 cups) finely ground almond flour

57 grams (½ cup) tapioca starch, plus more for shaping

2 teaspoons baking soda

½ teaspoon salt

2 large eggs (about 100 grams out of the shell)

2 tablespoons olive oil, plus more for topping focaccia

1 tablespoon apple cider vinegar

Kosher salt, to taste

About 2 teaspoons dried herbs, such as basil, oregano, rosemary, or thyme

Crushed red pepper (optional)

Preheat the oven to 425°F. Spray an 8-inch cast-iron skillet* with nonstick cooking spray or brush with melted coconut oil.

Whisk the almond flour, tapioca starch, baking soda, and salt together in a medium mixing bowl. Add the eggs and olive oil and stir with a wooden spoon until the dough holds together.

Add the vinegar and stir until the vinegar is completely absorbed. It's normal for the dough to fizz a little.

Place the dough in the prepared skillet. Generously dust your hands with tapioca starch and press the dough evenly into the skillet. Dip the handle of a clean, dry wooden spoon in tapioca starch and use it to dimple the dough all over. Brush generously with olive oil. Sprinkle the kosher salt, herbs, and crushed pepper over the top of the focaccia.

Bake until golden brown, about 20 minutes.

Remove the skillet from the oven. Allow the focaccia to cool in the pan for 5 minutes before serving.

. . . .

Focaccia is best enjoyed the day it's baked.

. . . .

* Don't have a cast-iron skillet? Make this in a greased 8-inch round cake pan.

Naan

Chewy, flavorful naan is the perfect bread for soaking up sauces and curries. At my house, only crumbs are left by the end of a meal.

Active Time: 30 minutes
Cook Time: about 4 minutes per bread
Yield: 6 flatbreads

170 grams (1 ½ cups) finely ground almond flour

57 grams (½ cup) tapioca starch, plus more for kneading

14 grams (2 tablespoons) coconut flour

2 ½ teaspoons baking powder, homemade (page 210) or grain-free store-bought

½ teaspoon salt

28 grams (2 tablespoons) coconut oil, melted and cooled slightly, plus more for cooking

2 large eggs (about 100 grams out of the shell)

Whisk the almond flour, ½ cup tapioca starch, coconut flour, baking powder, and salt together in a medium mixing bowl. Stir in the melted coconut oil and eggs with a wooden spoon. Cover dough with plastic wrap and allow to rest for 5 minutes.

Dust the counter with 1 tablespoon tapioca starch. Turn the dough out onto the counter and knead it until firm. The dough should not stick to your hands. Sprinkle with more tapioca starch if it does. (Depending on the humidity of the day, sometimes you need a little more tapioca starch and sometimes you need a lot.)

Pat the dough into a circle and cut it into six equal pieces. Lightly dust your counter with tapioca starch. Round each piece of dough and roll into a circle about 5 inches across.

Heat a cast-iron griddle or 10-inch cast-iron pan* over medium-high heat. Brush the griddle with a little melted coconut oil.

When the griddle is hot but not smoking, place the naan on it. Don't crowd them. On a large griddle, cook two or three at a time; in a skillet, cook one at a time.

Flip the bread when the surface bubbles and puffs, after about 3 minutes. Cook until golden brown on the second side, about 1 minute. Repeat with the remaining dough.

. . . .
Naan is best enjoyed as soon as it's cooked.
. . . .

* If you don't own a cast-iron griddle or 10-inch skillet, you can use an 8-inch nonstick frying pan. Naan cooked in a nonstick pan won't be as dark or puff as much as bread cooked in cast iron, but it'll still taste great.

Quick Pizza Crust `coconut-free`

I make pizza almost every Friday night. Several years ago, I switched from a yeast-based crust to a quick baking powder crust. This simple recipe can be made in the time it takes to preheat the oven.

Active Time: 20 minutes
Bake Time: 20 minutes (without toppings)
Yield: 2 (8-inch) personal pizzas or 1 (12 by 16-inch) family-size pizza

113 grams (1 cup) finely ground almond flour

113 grams (1 cup) tapioca starch, plus more for dusting

2 teaspoons baking powder, homemade (page 210) or grain-free store-bought

½ teaspoon salt

2 large eggs (about 100 grams out of the shell)

Adjust an oven rack to the middle position and preheat the oven to 350°F.

Whisk the almond flour, tapioca starch, baking powder, and salt together in a large mixing bowl. Add the eggs and stir with a wooden spoon until a thick, sticky dough holds together, about 30 minutes. Cover the bowl with plastic wrap and allow dough to rest for 10 minutes.

Generously dust the counter with tapioca starch. Turn the dough out onto the counter and knead it until smooth, about 1 minute. If the dough remains sticky, add more tapioca starch.

For two personal pizzas, grease two 8-inch cake pans with nonstick cooking spray or brush with melted coconut oil. Cut the dough in half. Roll out each piece into a 6-inch round. Transfer the dough to a prepared pan. With your hands, press out the dough to fill the pan. Repeat with the remaining dough. Bake the crusts until golden brown, about 20 minutes.

For a family-size pizza, place dough on a 12 by 16-inch piece of parchment paper. Roll out the dough until it almost covers the parchment paper. Grasp the parchment by the edges and in one swift motion, slide it onto a rimmed baking sheet.

Bake until lightly golden brown, about 20 minutes.

Remove the baked crust(s) from the oven, top as desired, and return to the oven until the topping is cooked through.

. . . .
Store leftover pizza in the refrigerator, wrapped, for up to 2 days. Reheat in a dry skillet over medium heat until warm.
. . . .

BAKER'S NOTE: *Bake First, Top Later*
Always bake the crust before topping it. This keeps the crust crisp.

Fresh Pasta Dough `coconut-free`

What's a recipe for pasta doing in a baking book? Well, baked goods and pasta both start with dough!

My favorite way to enjoy this is with a generous drizzle of fruity olive oil, a little bit of freshly minced garlic, and a sprinkle of lemon zest. Finish it with a good pinch of salt and you'll see why I love it so much.

Active Time: 45 minutes
Cook Time: about 5 minutes
Yield: 4 to 6 servings

142 grams (1 ¼ cups) tapioca starch, plus more for kneading and rolling

113 grams (1 cup) finely ground almond flour

½ teaspoon salt

2 large eggs (about 100 grams out of the shell)

2 tablespoons water*

* In the summer, when it's humid, this dough tends to be damp and the water isn't needed. In the winter, when it's dry, you'll probably need it.

Whisk the tapioca starch, almond flour, and salt together in a large mixing bowl. Add the eggs and stir with a wooden spoon until a thick, sticky dough holds together. If the dough is dry and crumbly, add the water one tablespoon at a time until the dough holds together.

Cover the dough with a piece of plastic wrap and allow it to rest for 10 minutes. This is important because it allows the dough to thicken. Without the rest, it's hard to work with.

Generously dust the counter with tapioca starch. Turn the dough out onto the counter and dust the top generously with tapioca starch. Knead the dough until smooth. If it is sticky, knead in more tapioca starch.

Bring a large pot of salted water (about 5 quarts water and 2 teaspoons salt) to a boil. Dust a rimmed baking sheet lightly with tapioca starch. Dust the counter again with tapioca starch.

Divide the dough into two equal pieces. Work with one piece at a time, keeping the other covered with plastic wrap or a dry kitchen towel. Press the dough to flatten it slightly. Roll the dough out into a large rectangle until it's about ⅛-inch thick. Using a pizza wheel, cut the dough into ½-inch-wide strips. Gently gather up the strips of pasta and transfer to the prepared baking sheet. Repeat with the remaining dough.

Cook the pasta in the boiling water, stirring gently from time to time, until tender, about 5 minutes. Drain and serve immediately with your choice of sauce.

Pasta is best enjoyed immediately after it's cooked.

Savory Dinner Muffins `almond-free`

In the winter, these muffins are great with a big bowl of chili. In the summer, serve them with an antipasto platter or large salad.

Active Time: 15 minutes
Bake Time: 25 minutes
Yield: 6 muffins

67 grams (⅓ cup) plus 1 teaspoon olive oil

½ small onion, diced (¼ cup)

1 garlic clove, minced or put through a garlic press

57 grams (½ cup) coconut flour

1 ½ teaspoons baking powder, homemade (page 210) or grain-free store-bought

1 teaspoon freshly ground black pepper

½ teaspoon crushed red pepper

½ teaspoon salt

4 large eggs (about 200 grams out of the shell)

Adjust an oven rack to the middle position. Preheat the oven to 350°F. Line 6 standard-size muffin cups with paper liners.

Heat 1 teaspoon of the olive oil in an 8-inch nonstick frying pan over medium heat. Add the onion and cook until soft, about 3 minutes, stirring frequently. Add the garlic and cook until soft, about another minute. Remove from the heat and allow to cool.

Whisk the coconut flour, baking powder, black pepper, crushed pepper, and salt together in a medium mixing bowl. Add the eggs and the remaining ⅓ cup olive oil and whisk until smooth. Stir in the onion and garlic. The batter will be thick. Scoop the batter into the prepared muffin cups, filling each cup about two-thirds full.

Bake until the muffins are golden brown and spring back to the touch, about 25 minutes.

Allow the muffins to cool in the pan for 5 minutes, then remove from pan and place on a wire rack to cool. Serve the muffins warm or allow them to cool completely.

· ·

These muffins are best enjoyed the day they are baked. Wrap cooled leftovers with plastic wrap and store at room temperature for 1 day.

· ·

Garlic, Onion, and Herb Waffles

coconut-free

These waffles are perfect for those times you want something savory with your eggs and bacon. I also love them served along with dinner.

Active Time: 15 minutes
Cook Time: varies depending on the waffle iron
Yield: about 4 Belgian waffles or 6 regular waffles, depending on the size of the waffle maker

2 tablespoons plus 1 teaspoon olive oil

1 small onion, finely chopped (about ⅓ cup)

1 medium garlic clove, minced or put through a garlic press

142 grams (1 ¼ cups) finely ground almond flour

57 grams (½ cup) tapioca starch

2 teaspoons baking powder, homemade (page 210) or grain-free store-bought

½ teaspoon salt

¼ teaspoon freshly ground black pepper*

¼ teaspoon dried rosemary** or ½ teaspoon chopped fresh rosemary

113 grams (½ cup) milk, dairy-free or traditional

1 large egg (about 50 grams out of the shell)

* Increase the pepper to ½ teaspoon for a more intense flavor.

** After you measure the dried rosemary, lightly rub it between your finger and thumb as you drop it into the bowl. This breaks it up a little and releases flavor.

Heat 1 teaspoon of the olive oil in an 8-inch nonstick frying pan over medium heat. Add the onion and cook until soft and translucent, about 2 minutes, stirring frequently. Add the garlic and cook until soft, about 1 minute. Remove from the heat and allow to cool slightly.

Preheat the waffle iron.

Whisk the almond flour, tapioca starch, baking powder, salt, black pepper, and rosemary together in a medium mixing bowl. Add the milk, egg, and the remaining 2 tablespoons olive oil and whisk until smooth. Add the onions and garlic and whisk until combined.

Lightly grease the waffle iron with nonstick cooking spray or brush with melted coconut oil. Pour batter into the iron as directed by the manufacturer. Bake until the waffles are brown and crisp. Repeat with the remaining batter.

· ·

Waffles are best enjoyed as soon as they are baked, but they also freeze well. Allow the waffles to cool. Stack them with pieces of parchment or waxed paper in between. Slide the stack into a freezer bag, seal, and freeze up to 2 weeks. When you are in the mood for waffles, thaw them in 30-second intervals in the microwave until warm.

· ·

Hogs in a Sweater `almond-free`

Inspired by corn dogs, these savory mini-muffins make a simple supper. I like to serve them on game day with a big green salad.

Active Time: 15 minutes
Bake Time: about 18 minutes
Yield: 24 mini muffins

57 grams (½ cup) coconut flour

1 ½ teaspoons baking powder, homemade (page 210) or grain-free store-bought

½ teaspoon salt

4 large eggs (about 200 grams out of the shell)

67 grams (⅓ cup) olive oil

4 gluten-free, grain-free hot dogs,* each cut into six pieces

* I like Applegate Farms grain-free, grass-fed beef hot dogs.

Adjust an oven rack to the middle position and preheat the oven to 350°F. Spray 1 mini-muffin pan (24 muffin cups) with nonstick cooking spray.

Whisk the coconut flour, baking powder, and salt together in a medium mixing bowl. Add the eggs and oil and whisk until smooth. Spoon about 1 tablespoon batter into each muffin cup and press one hot dog piece into the center of each.

Bake until golden brown, about 18 minutes. Serve warm.

• •

Hogs in a sweater are best enjoyed the day they are baked. Wrap leftovers with plastic wrap and store in the refrigerator for up to a day. Heat in 30-second intervals in the microwave until warm.

• •

Not-So-Common Crackers `coconut-free`

In New England, "common crackers" are, well, common. Heartier than a saltine, they resemble small, dry, crisp biscuits. I love them in a bowl of soup. The first time I made a batch of these, my husband Greg said, "Oh! You made common crackers!" He didn't even realize they were grain-free.

Be sure to roll out the dough very thin; that's an important step if you want a crisp cracker. For ease, I cut mine into squares with a pizza cutter. These are easy enough to make that you can whip up a batch while a pot of chicken soup bubbles on the stove.

Active Time: 20 minutes
Bake Time: 15 minutes
Yield: about 36 crackers

113 grams (1 cup) finely ground almond flour

113 grams (1 cup) tapioca starch, plus more for kneading

½ teaspoon baking powder, homemade (page 210) or grain-free store-bought

½ teaspoon salt

2 large eggs (about 100 grams out of the shell)

Kosher salt

Adjust an oven rack to the middle position and preheat the oven to 425°F.

Whisk the almond flour, tapioca starch, baking powder, and salt together in a medium mixing bowl. Stir in the eggs with a wooden spoon. The dough will be stiff.

Generously dust the counter with tapioca starch. Turn the dough out onto the counter and knead it until it's no longer sticky. Add more tapioca starch as needed.

Place the dough on a 12 by 16-inch piece of parchment paper. Lightly dust the top of the dough with tapioca starch. Cover the dough with a second piece of parchment paper. Roll out the dough to a 9 by 13-inch rectangle. Peel off the top piece of parchment. Do this slowly or the dough might stick and tear.

Score the dough into small rectangles, about 1 by 1 ½ inches, using a pizza wheel. This makes it easier to cut when it comes out of the oven. Don't try to move the crackers apart. Prick the dough all over with a fork. Sprinkle with kosher salt. Grasp the parchment by the edges and, in one swift motion, slide it onto a rimmed baking sheet.

Bake until golden brown, about 15 minutes.

As soon as you remove the crackers from the oven, use the pizza cutter to go back over the score lines. Allow the crackers to cool on the pan.

• •
Store crackers on the counter in an airtight container for up to 4 days.
• •

Flour Tortillas `coconut-free`

This recipe challenged everything I knew about making tortillas. I tried (and tried and tried) to make a grain-free tortilla using a tortilla press. The dough never worked quite right. Then I went against everything I knew; you could say I went "against the grain." Ahem. Instead of trying to make a rollable dough, I made one that was crepe-batter loose. I poured the thin batter into a nonstick frying pan and quickly rotated the pan. The crepe method worked. These flour tortillas are flavorful and foldable. Fill them with whatever you love.

Active Time: about 15 minutes
Cook Time: about 3 minutes per tortilla
Yield: 6 tortillas

57 grams (½ cup) finely ground almond flour

57 grams (½ cup) tapioca starch

½ teaspoon salt

1 large egg (about 50 grams out of the shell)

60 grams (¼ cup) water

Whisk the almond flour, tapioca starch, and salt together in a medium mixing bowl. Add the egg and water and whisk until smooth.

Lightly grease an 8-inch nonstick frying pan with nonstick cooking spray or brush with melted coconut oil. Heat the pan over medium heat until hot but not smoking. Pour ¼ cup batter into the pan. Lift the pan from the burner and quickly rotate the pan to spread the batter out.

Place the pan back down on the burner. Cook until the batter is set. It will look flat, and the bottom side will brown. Flip and cook another minute or so, until the other side is golden brown. Transfer the tortilla to a plate. Place a piece of waxed paper between each tortilla to prevent them from sticking. Repeat with the remaining batter. Serve warm or cool.

. . . .
Tortillas are best enjoyed the day they are cooked.
. . . .

Sandwich Wraps `almond-free`

After creating the almond-flour tortilla recipe, I wanted something a little different to use as a sandwich wrap. This recipe, which uses coconut flour instead, makes incredibly tender wraps. I use them for a variety of roll-ups, my favorite being turkey and ham.

Active Time: about 30 minutes
Cook Time: about 4 minutes per wrap
Yield: 6 wraps

57 grams (½ cup) tapioca starch

21 grams (3 tablespoons) coconut flour

½ teaspoon salt

2 large eggs (about 100 grams out of the shell)

113 grams (½ cup) water

Whisk the tapioca starch, coconut flour, and salt together in a medium mixing bowl. Add the eggs and water and whisk until smooth. Allow the batter to rest for 3 minutes.

Lightly grease an 8-inch nonstick frying pan with nonstick cooking spray or brush with melted coconut oil. Heat the pan over medium heat until hot but not smoking. Pour ¼ cup batter into the pan. Lift the pan from the burner and quickly rotate the pan to spread the batter out.

Place the pan back down on the burner. Cook until the batter is set. It will look flat, and the bottom side will be golden brown. Flip and cook another minute or so, until the other side is golden brown. Transfer the wrap to a plate. Place a piece of waxed paper between each wrap to prevent them from sticking together. Repeat with remaining batter. Serve when cool.

· ·
Sandwich wraps are best enjoyed the day they are cooked.
· ·

Cookies and Bars

The Best Chocolate Chip Cookies

Soft Chocolate Chip Cookies

Paleos (Chocolate Sandwich Cookies)

Snickerdoodles

Gingersnaps

Maple Softies

Pinkie Print Cookies

The World's Easiest Cookies

Loaded-with-Good-Things Cookies

Cut-Out Cookies

Magic Cut-Out Cookies

Honey Grahamless Crackers

Fudge Brownies

Chocolate Chip Cookie Bars

The World's Easiest Blondies

Tart Lemon Bars

Paleos (Chocolate Sandwich Cookies), page 96

The Best Chocolate Chip Cookies

`coconut-free`

All hail the king of cookies! This version is a delicious new take on everyone's favorite, the chocolate chip cookie. The coconut sugar lends a nutty flavor that I adore. And speaking of nutty, go ahead and stir in a half-cup of your favorite chopped nuts. Walnuts are a traditional addition, but any tree nut will work.

Active Time: about 10 minutes
Bake Time: about 10 minutes per pan
Yield: 12 cookies

142 grams (1 ¼ cups) finely ground almond flour

28 grams (¼ cup) tapioca starch

1 teaspoon baking powder, homemade (page 210) or grain-free store-bought

½ teaspoon salt

3 tablespoons honey

2 tablespoons dark maple syrup

1 large egg yolk (about 15 grams)

1 teaspoon vanilla extract

113 grams (½ cup) dairy-free dark chocolate chips or chopped dark chocolate

Adjust an oven rack to the middle position and preheat the oven to 350°F. Line a rimmed baking sheet with parchment paper.

Whisk the almond flour, tapioca starch, baking powder, and salt together in a medium mixing bowl. Add the honey, maple syrup, egg yolk, and vanilla and stir with a wooden spoon to combine. Stir in the chocolate chips.

Drop dough by the tablespoonful onto the prepared baking sheet, spaced about 2 inches apart to allow for spreading.

Bake until golden brown, about 10 minutes.

Allow the cookies to cool on the pan for 5 minutes, then transfer them to a wire rack to cool completely.

Allow the baking sheet to cool, and repeat with the remaining dough.

. . . .
Store on the counter in an airtight container for up to 4 days, or freeze, wrapped in plastic wrap and placed in a freezer container, for up to 6 weeks.
. . . .

Soft Chocolate Chip Cookies

For a child of the 1980s, boxes of soft chocolate chip cookies were always served at school birthday parties. While they aren't quite as popular as they once were, I'm still fond of them. Chocolate and childhood joy? What more could you want from a cookie?

Active Time: 20 minutes
Bake Time: about 10 minutes per pan
Yield: 16 cookies

36 grams (⅓ cup) coconut flour

½ teaspoon baking powder, homemade (page 210) or grain-free store-bought

½ teaspoon salt

57 grams (¼ cup) coconut oil, solid, or unsalted butter, softened

85 grams (½ cup) coconut sugar or evaporated cane juice

2 large eggs (about 100 grams out of the shell)

1 teaspoon vanilla extract

85 grams (½ cup) dairy-free mini dark chocolate chips or finely chopped dark chocolate

Adjust an oven rack to the middle position and preheat the oven to 350°F. Line a rimmed baking sheet with parchment paper.

Whisk the coconut flour, baking powder, and salt together in a small mixing bowl. Combine the coconut oil and coconut sugar in a medium mixing bowl. With a handheld mixer set on medium speed, beat until a thick paste forms. Stop the mixer and add the eggs and vanilla. Turn the mixer to medium and beat until light. Add the dry ingredients and mix until the dough holds together. Add the chocolate chips and mix until incorporated.

Drop dough in heaping teaspoons onto the prepared baking sheet, spaced about 2 inches apart to allow for spreading.

Bake until set and dark golden brown, about 10 minutes.

Allow the cookies to cool on the pan on a wire rack for 5 minutes, and then transfer them directly to the rack to cool completely.

Allow the baking sheet to cool, and repeat with the remaining dough.

· ·

These cookies are best enjoyed the day they are baked. Freeze leftover cookies for up to 1 month.

· ·

Paleos (Chocolate Sandwich Cookies) `starch-free`

If chocolate chip cookies are king, then chocolate sandwich cookies are queen! When you are in the mood for something a little different, the variation made with peppermint oil makes a cool treat.

In the early 1990s, Nabisco replaced the lard in their OREO cookies with vegetable shortening. I preferred the lard. If you don't keep lard in the house, make the filling with either palm shortening or butter. Coconut oil doesn't work because it will melt if the temperature gets higher than 76°F.

Active Time: 20 minutes
Bake Time: about 10 minutes per pan
Yield: 24 sandwich cookies

Cookies

170 grams (1 ½ cups) finely ground almond flour

85 grams (½ cup) coconut sugar or evaporated cane juice

38 grams (¼ cup plus 2 tablespoons) Dutch-process cocoa powder, plus additional for dusting

21 grams (3 tablespoons) coconut flour

½ teaspoon baking soda

½ teaspoon salt

57 grams (¼ cup) coconut oil, solid, or unsalted butter, softened

1 large egg (about 50 grams out of the shell)

1 tablespoon milk, dairy-free or traditional

Vanilla Crème Filling

113 grams (½ cup) lard, palm shortening or butter, at room temperature

226 grams (2 cups) powdered sugar, homemade (page 210) or grain-free store-bought

1 tablespoon milk, dairy-free or traditional

1 teaspoon vanilla extract

Adjust an oven rack to the middle position and preheat the oven to 350°F. Line a rimmed baking sheet with parchment paper.

To make the dough in a food processor: Combine the almond flour, coconut sugar, cocoa powder, coconut flour, baking soda, and salt in the food processor. Pulse a few times to combine. Add the coconut oil and pulse until no large pieces of coconut oil remain, six or seven pulses. Add the egg and milk. Run the food processor for about 30 seconds. Don't process for too long or the oil will run out of the dough.

To mix the dough by hand: Combine the almond flour, coconut sugar, cocoa powder, coconut flour, baking soda, and salt in a large mixing bowl. Whisk to combine. Add the coconut oil. Use a pastry cutter or your fingers to cut the coconut oil into the dry ingredients until the mixture resembles coarse meal. You don't want any large nubs of coconut oil. (If you use your fingers, work in the coconut oil with a quick snapping motion.) Stir in the egg and milk with a wooden spoon. Mix until a stiff dough holds together.

Place a 12 by 16-inch piece of parchment paper on the counter and dust it lightly with cocoa powder. Turn the dough out onto the parchment and dust the top with cocoa powder. Cover the dough with a second piece of parchment. Roll the dough out to a ⅛-inch thickness. Cut the dough into rounds with a 1 ¾-inch cutter. Transfer the cookies to the prepared baking sheet. You can place the cookies fairly close together, because the dough doesn't spread.

Bake until the cookies are set and aromatic, about 10 minutes.

Allow the cookies to cool on the pan for 5 minutes, then transfer them to a wire rack to cool completely.

Allow the baking sheet to cool. Reroll the remaining dough (it doesn't contain gluten and won't get tough when rerolled) and repeat as directed above.

While the cookies are cooling, make the filling: Combine the lard, powdered sugar, milk, and vanilla in a large mixing bowl. Using a handheld mixer on medium speed, beat until thick and creamy.

Sandwich the cooled cookies together with about 1 ½ teaspoons of filling each. (If you sandwich warm cookies together with the filling, the filling will get warm and runny.)

. . . .

Store cookies in an airtight container on the counter for up to four days. Freeze, wrapped in plastic wrap and placed in a freezer container (or wrapped in plastic wrap and then again in foil), for up to 6 weeks.

. . . .

Variation

Peppermint Paleos: Add ¼ teaspoon pure peppermint oil (not peppermint extract) to the dough along with the milk.

Snickerdoodles

`egg free; coconut-free if made with butter`

Snickerdoodles are something of a New England classic. They're vanilla cookies rolled in cinnamon sugar. Like so many things in baking, the whole is greater than the sum of the parts. Much more than simple sugar cookies, they're delicate, spicy, and sweet.

Active Time: 15 minutes
Bake Time: about 10 minutes per pan
Yield: 12 cookies

Dough

170 grams (1 ½ cups) finely ground almond flour

57 grams (½ cup) tapioca starch

½ teaspoon baking powder, homemade (page 210) or grain-free store-bought

¼ teaspoon salt

57 grams (¼ cup) coconut oil, solid, or unsalted butter, chilled

113 grams (⅓ cup) honey

1 teaspoon vanilla extract

Cinnamon Sugar

2 tablespoons granulated maple sugar

1 teaspoon ground cinnamon

Adjust an oven rack to the middle position and preheat the oven to 350°F. Line a rimmed baking sheet with parchment paper.

To make the dough in a food processor: Combine the almond flour, tapioca starch, baking powder, and salt in the food processor. Pulse a few times to combine. Add the coconut oil and pulse until no large pieces of oil remain, about four long pulses. Add the honey and vanilla and pulse to combine. Run the food processor for about 20 seconds. A ball of dough might form or the mixture might look crumbly. Either is fine. You just don't want to process the dough for so long that the oil runs out of it. If a ball of dough does not form, turn the dough out the counter and knead it a few times until it holds together.

Transfer the dough to a medium mixing bowl.

To mix the dough by hand: Whisk the almond flour, tapioca starch, baking powder, and salt together in a large mixing bowl. Add the coconut oil. Use a pastry cutter or your fingers to cut the coconut oil into the dry ingredients until the mixture resembles coarse meal. You don't want any large nubs of coconut oil. If you use your fingers, work in the coconut oil with a quick snapping motion. Stir in the honey and vanilla with a wooden spoon, until a stiff dough holds together.

Whisk the maple sugar and cinnamon together in a small bowl.

Scoop out about 2 teaspoons dough for each cookie and shape into balls. Roll the balls in the cinnamon sugar. Place the balls on the prepared baking sheet about 2 inches apart.

Bake until golden brown, about 10 minutes.

Allow the cookies to cool on the pan for 5 minutes before transferring them to a wire rack to cool completely.

Allow the baking sheet to cool, and repeat with the remaining dough.

- -

Wrap cookies in plastic wrap and store on the counter for up to 3 days, or freeze, wrapped in plastic wrap and placed in a freezer container, for up to 1 month.

- -

Gingersnaps

egg free; coconut-free if made with butter

Bags of sturdy gingersnaps were a part of my childhood. Often when my mom unpacked the groceries, she'd put a brown bag of gingersnaps in the pantry, chuckle and say, "These must have followed me home." Since they were always around, I never thought of gingersnaps as a winter-only treat. In the summer, try a few with a glass of peach iced tea. You'll love it, I promise.

Active Time: 15 minutes
Bake Time: about 10 minutes
Yield: 12 cookies

198 grams (1 ¾ cups) finely ground almond flour

28 grams (¼ cup) tapioca starch

2 teaspoons ground ginger

1 teaspoon ground cinnamon

½ teaspoon baking soda

¼ teaspoon ground cloves

¼ teaspoon salt

57 grams (¼ cup) coconut oil, solid, or unsalted butter, chilled

85 grams (¼ cup) unsulphured molasses or dark maple syrup

1 teaspoon vanilla extract

Adjust an oven rack to the middle position and preheat the oven to 350°F. Line a rimmed baking sheet with parchment paper.

To make the dough in a food processor: Combine the almond flour, tapioca starch, ginger, cinnamon, baking soda, cloves, and salt in the food processor. Pulse a few times to combine. Add the coconut oil and pulse until no large pieces of oil remain, about four long pulses. Add the molasses and vanilla and pulse to combine. Run the food processor for about 20 seconds. A ball of dough might form, or the mixture might look crumbly. Either is fine. You just don't want to process the dough for so long that the oil runs out of it. If the mixture is still crumbly, turn it out onto the counter and knead it a few times, until it holds together.

Transfer the dough to a medium mixing bowl.

To mix the dough by hand: Whisk the almond flour, tapioca starch, ginger, cinnamon, baking soda, cloves, and salt together in a large mixing bowl. Add the coconut oil. Use a pastry cutter or your fingers to cut the coconut oil into the dry ingredients until the mixture resembles coarse meal. You don't want any large nubs of coconut oil. If you use your fingers, work in the coconut oil with a quick snapping motion. Stir in the molasses and vanilla with a wooden spoon. Mix until a stiff dough holds together.

Scoop out about 2 teaspoons of dough for each cookie and shape into balls. Place the balls on the prepared baking sheet about 2 inches apart. Press down each ball with the flat bottom of a glass or measuring cup until they are about ¾-inch thick.

Bake until golden brown, about 10 minutes.

Allow the cookies to cool on the pan for 5 minutes before transferring them to a wire rack to cool completely.

Wrap the cookies in plastic wrap and store on the counter for up to 3 days, or freeze, wrapped in plastic wrap and placed in a freezer container, for up to 1 month.

Maple Softies

While attempting to create a recipe for snickerdoodles, I accidently created these soft maple cookies. My reaction? "These are terrible snickerdoodles . . . but awesome maple cookies!" If you don't like maple, swap the granulated maple sugar for granulated honey and the maple syrup for liquid honey. You'll make honey softies, which sounds like both a term of endearment and a tasty cookie.

Active Time: 20 minutes
Bake Time: 10 minutes per pan
Yield: about 16 cookies

113 grams (1 cup) finely ground almond flour

28 grams (¼ cup) coconut flour

28 grams (¼ cup) tapioca starch

¾ teaspoon baking powder, homemade (page 210) or grain-free store-bought

½ teaspoon ground cinnamon

½ teaspoon salt

75 grams (⅓ cup) coconut oil, solid, or unsalted butter, softened

42 grams (¼ cup) granulated maple sugar

75 grams (¼ cup) dark maple syrup

2 large eggs (about 100 grams out of the shell)

Adjust an oven rack to the middle position and preheat the oven to 350°F. Line a rimmed baking sheet with parchment paper.

Whisk the almond flour, coconut flour, tapioca starch, baking powder, cinnamon, and salt together in a small mixing bowl. Beat together the coconut oil, maple sugar, and maple syrup in a medium mixing bowl, using a handheld mixer set on medium speed. Add the eggs one at a time, and beat until fluffy. Stop the mixer and scrape the bottom and sides of the bowl with a rubber spatula. Add the dry ingredients and mix on medium-low speed, until a dough forms.

Drop the dough by the tablespoonful onto the prepared baking sheet, spaced about 2 inches apart to allow for spreading. Bake until cookies are set and golden brown, about 10 minutes. Allow the cookies to cool on the pan for 3 minutes, then transfer them to a wire rack to cool completely.

Allow baking sheet to cool, and repeat with remaining dough.

• •

Store on the counter in an airtight container for up to 3 days, or freeze, wrapped in plastic wrap and placed in a freezer container, for up to 6 weeks.

• •

Variation

Maple Walnut Softies: Stir 85 grams (¾ cup) chopped walnuts into the batter.

Pinkie Print Cookies

egg-free; coconut-free

Dainty and filled with a hint of jam, these cookies are great with a cup of hot tea. For fun, try using a few different jams—blueberry, cherry, and raspberry—per batch.

Active Time: 20 minutes
Bake Time: about 9 minutes per pan
Yield: 36 cookies

170 grams (1 ½ cups) finely ground almond flour

57 grams (½ cup) tapioca starch

½ teaspoon baking powder, homemade (page 210) or grain-free store-bought

½ teaspoon salt

85 grams (¼ cup) honey

About ¼ cup jam*

* If possible, use homemade or locally made jam. If that's not an option, be sure to select a jam that does not include corn syrup.

Adjust an oven rack to the middle position and preheat the oven to 350°F. Line a rimmed baking sheet with parchment paper.

Whisk almond flour, tapioca starch, baking powder, and salt together in a medium mixing bowl. Add the honey and stir with a wooden spoon until a thick dough holds together.

Scoop out about 2 teaspoons of dough for each cookie and shape into balls. Place on the prepared baking sheet about 2 inches apart. Using your pinkie, make a small depression in the center of each cookie. Spoon a small amount of jam into each depression.

Bake until the cookies are set and golden brown, about 9 minutes.

Allow the cookies to cool on the pan for 3 minutes, then transfer them to a wire rack to cool completely. Be careful; the jam remains really hot for a bit and can burn your mouth.

Allow the baking sheet to cool, and repeat with the remaining dough.

· ·

Wrap in plastic wrap and store on the counter for up to 3 days, or freeze, wrapped in plastic wrap and placed in a freezer container, for up to 1 month. Place pieces of waxed paper between the cookie layers to prevent the jam from sticking.

· ·

The World's Easiest Cookies

`egg-free; coconut-free`

If I hadn't baked these cookies myself, I might read the recipe and think it's missing something. But it's not! Made with only four ingredients, these cookies are a nice, easy option when you want a little something sweet and delicious.

You can make either crisp cookies or ones that are soft in the center. I think you'll need to bake two batches to see which you prefer, don't you?

Active Time: 5 minutes
Bake Time: 12 minutes per pan
Yield: 16 cookies

227 grams (2 cups) finely ground almond flour

½ teaspoon baking powder, homemade (page 210) or grain-free store-bought

100 grams (⅓ cup) dark maple syrup

2 teaspoons vanilla extract

Adjust an oven rack to the middle position and preheat the oven to 350°F. Line a rimmed baking sheet with parchment paper.

Whisk the almond flour and baking powder together in a medium mixing bowl. Switch to a wooden spoon and stir in the maple syrup and vanilla. Stir until a sticky dough holds together.

Drop dough by the tablespoonful onto the prepared baking sheet, spaced about 2 inches apart to allow for spreading. For crisp cookies, press down the dough lightly with the flat bottom of a drinking glass or measuring cup. (If the glass sticks to the dough, dip the bottom in tapioca starch.) For softer cookies, don't press down the dough.

Bake until the edges are golden brown, about 12 minutes.

Allow the cookies to cool on the pan for about 3 minutes, then transfer them to a wire rack to cool completely.

Allow the baking sheet to cool, and repeat with the remaining dough.

. . . .
Store on the counter in an airtight container for up to 3 days, or freeze, wrapped in plastic wrap and placed in a freezer container, for up to 6 weeks.
. . . .

Loaded-with-Good-Things Cookies

coconut-free

"Too much of a good thing can be wonderful!"—Mae West

Chocolate chips? Check. Nuts? Yup. Dried fruit? Got it. These cookies have them all with just enough dough to hold everything together.

Active Time: 15 minutes
Bake Time: about 15 minutes per pan
Yield: 12 cookies

142 grams (1 ¼ cups) finely ground almond flour

28 grams (¼ cup) tapioca starch

1 teaspoon baking powder, homemade (page 210) or grain-free store-bought

½ teaspoon salt

1 large egg (about 50 grams out of the shell)

3 tablespoons honey

2 tablespoons dark maple syrup

1 teaspoon vanilla extract

70 grams (½ cup) chopped dairy-free dark chocolate

70 grams (½ cup) chopped dried fruit (see Baker's Note, page 193)

70 grams (½ cup) chopped nuts

Adjust an oven rack to the middle position and preheat the oven to 350°F. Line a rimmed baking sheet with parchment paper.

Whisk the almond flour, tapioca starch, baking powder, and salt together in a medium mixing bowl. Switch to a wooden spoon and stir in the egg, honey, maple syrup, and vanilla. Allow the dough to rest for about 5 minutes.

Stir in the chocolate, fruit, and nuts.

Drop dough by the tablespoonful onto the prepared baking sheet, spaced about 2 inches apart to allow for spreading.

Bake until the edges are golden brown, about 15 minutes.

Allow the cookies to cool on the pan for 3 minutes, then transfer them to a wire rack to cool completely.

Allow the baking sheet to cool, and repeat with the remaining dough.

. . . .

Store on the counter in an airtight container for up to 3 days, or freeze, wrapped in plastic wrap and placed in a freezer container, for up to 6 weeks.

. . . .

Cut-Out Cookies `coconut-free if made with butter`

I own at least 100 cookie cutters. Every time I think about paring it down, I remember that my odd-ball collection contains everything from stars to a dachshund to an armadillo. And who can part with an armadillo cutter? Not me.

No matter what shape you cut these cookies, make sure the dough warms up a little before rolling it. If the dough cracks as you roll, that means it's too cold. If it sticks to the counter, it's too warm. Oh, and those cutters? Dip them in tapioca starch before cutting out shapes; it keeps the dough from sticking to the cutter.

Active Time: 20 minutes
Chill Time: 1 hour
Bake Time: about 10 minutes per pan
Yield: about 20 (4-inch) cookies

113 grams (1 cup) finely ground almond flour

113 grams (1 cup) tapioca starch

½ teaspoon baking powder, homemade (page 210) or grain-free store-bought

½ teaspoon salt

85 grams (½ cup) evaporated cane juice or coconut sugar

57 grams (¼ cup) coconut oil, solid, or unsalted butter, softened

1 large egg (about 50 grams out of the shell)

1 teaspoon vanilla extract

1 tablespoon water

Whisk the almond flour, tapioca starch, baking powder, and salt together in a small mixing bowl. Combine the evaporated cane juice and coconut oil in a medium mixing bowl. Use a handheld mixer set on medium speed to beat them until a thick paste forms. If there are any large lumps of coconut oil, stop the mixer and squeeze the paste together with your hand, or break up the lumps with a fork. Add the egg and mix until combined. Stop the mixer and add the dry ingredients, vanilla, and water. Mix until a dough forms.

Turn the dough out onto the counter. Knead gently a few times. Wrap the dough in plastic wrap and chill for 1 hour.

Adjust an oven rack to the middle position and preheat the oven to 325°F. Line a rimmed baking sheet with parchment paper.

Allow the dough to sit outside the refrigerator for about 10 minutes. Cut the dough in half and sprinkle your counter with a little tapioca starch. Roll out the dough about ¼-inch thick. Cut into shapes and place on prepared baking sheet about 2 inches apart.

Bake until set and golden brown, about 10 minutes for 4-inch cookies.

Allow the cookies to cool on the pan on a wire rack for 5 minutes, then transfer the cookies directly to the rack to cool completely.

Allow the baking sheet to cool. Reroll scraps and repeat with the remaining dough.

• •
Store on the counter in an airtight container for up to 4 days, or freeze, wrapped in plastic wrap and placed in a freezer container, for up to 6 weeks.
• •

Magic Cut-Out Cookies `egg-free; coconut-free`

This egg-free dough makes magical cookies. It's best made in a food processor. Take care not to overmix, or the dough will get oily from the almond flour. To avoid this, stop the processor after only a few pulses, then finish mixing the dough by squeezing it together with your hands. It's that simple!

These cookies spread a little during baking, so intricate cookie cutters aren't the best. Instead, select ones, like circles, that will hold their shape.

Active Time: 10 minutes
Chill Time: 2 hours
Bake Time: 10 minutes per pan
Yield: 24 (4-inch) cookies

170 grams (1 ½ cups) finely ground almond flour

57 grams (½ cup) tapioca starch

½ teaspoon salt

28 grams (2 tablespoons) coconut oil, solid or unsalted butter, softened

113 grams (⅓ cup) honey

1 teaspoon vanilla extract

Combine the almond flour, tapioca starch, and salt in a food processor. Pulse to combine. Add the coconut oil and pulse to combine. No large pieces of coconut oil should remain. Add the honey and vanilla and pulse to combine, about four pulses. The mixture will not form a ball of dough. This is fine.

Turn the mixture out onto the counter and knead until the dough holds together. Pat the dough into a round, wrap tightly with plastic wrap, and chill for 2 hours.

Adjust an oven rack to the middle position and preheat the oven to 325°F. Line a rimmed baking sheet with parchment paper.

Allow the dough to sit outside the refrigerator for about 10 minutes. Cut the dough in half and sprinkle your counter with a little tapioca starch. Roll out the dough about ¼-inch thick. Cut into shapes and place on the prepared baking sheet about 2 inches apart.

Bake until set and golden brown, about 10 minutes for 4-inch cookies.

Allow the cookies to cool on the pan on a wire rack for 5 minutes, then transfer the cookies directly to the rack to cool completely.

Allow the baking sheet to cool, and repeat with the remaining dough.

. . . .

Store on the counter in an airtight container for up to 4 days, or freeze, wrapped in plastic wrap and placed in a freezer container, for up to 6 weeks.

. . . .

Honey Grahamless Crackers

egg-free; coconut-free

S'mores. No-bake pie crusts. Sad days. Happy days. All are perfect occasions for graham crackers. The dough in this recipe comes together easily, with a bit of delicate handling. The hardest part is waiting for these treats to cool when they are fresh out of the oven.

Active Time: about 20 minutes
Bake Time: about 15 minutes
Yield: 12 crackers

142 grams (1 ¼ cups) finely ground almond flour

57 grams (½ cup) tapioca starch plus more for kneading

¼ teaspoon baking powder, homemade (page 210) or grain-free store-bought

¼ teaspoon salt

2 tablespoons honey

2 tablespoons milk

Adjust an oven rack to the middle position and preheat the oven to 350°F.

Whisk the almond flour, tapioca starch, baking powder, and salt together in a medium mixing bowl. Stir in the honey and milk with a wooden spoon. The dough will look very dry.

Turn the dough out onto the counter and knead it. After about 1 minute, the oils will release from the almond flour and the dough should hold together. If the dough is still too dry after 1 minute, knead in an additional tablespoon of milk. (Or, if your dough is too wet and sticky to knead, dust the counter with tapioca starch.)

Place the dough on a 12 by 16 inch piece of parchment paper. Dust the top of the dough with tapioca starch. Cover with a second piece of parchment paper. Roll out the dough into an 8 by 10-inch rectangle. Peel off the top piece of parchment. Do this slowly or the dough will tear.

Score the dough into 12 rectangles, using a pizza wheel. This makes it easier to cut when they are baked. Don't move the crackers apart. Prick the dough all over with a fork. Grasp the parchment by the edges and in one swift motion, slide it onto a rimmed baking sheet.

Bake until golden brown, about 15 minutes.

As soon as you remove the graham crackers from the oven, use the pizza cutter to go back over the score lines. Allow the crackers to cool on the pan.

• •
Store on the counter in an airtight container for up to 3 days, or freeze, wrapped in plastic wrap and placed in a freezer container, for up to 6 weeks.
• •

Fudge Brownies

Sometimes after a good workout, you want a sweet reward. This recipe gives you both! I like to refer to these as "triceps-busting brownies" because the thick batter is best mixed by hand with a wooden spoon. The work is worth it, though. You're rewarded with brownies that taste like a cross between the best chocolate cake you've ever had and a piece of decadent fudge.

Active Time: 15 minutes
Bake Time: 25 minutes
Yield: 9 brownies

57 grams (½ cup) finely ground almond flour

50 grams (½ cup) Dutch-process cocoa powder*

85 grams (½ cup) coconut sugar or evaporated cane juice

½ teaspoon baking powder, homemade (page 210) or grain-free store-bought

¼ teaspoon salt

113 grams (about ⅔ cup) chopped dairy-free dark chocolate or chips, melted (see Baker's Note, page 190)

57 grams (¼ cup) coconut oil or unsalted butter, melted and cooled slightly

85 grams (¼ cup) honey

3 large eggs (about 150 grams out of the shell)

* If you are unable to find Dutch-process cocoa powder, replace it with natural cocoa powder and replace the baking powder with ¼ teaspoon baking soda.

Adjust an oven rack to the middle position and preheat the oven to 325°F. Spray an 8-inch square cake pan with nonstick cooking spray. Cut a piece of parchment paper as wide as the pan and long enough to overhang the edges of the pan by 2 inches. Place the parchment in the pan, running your finger along the edge so it fits snuggly. Spray the parchment with nonstick cooking spray or brush with melted coconut oil.

Whisk the almond flour, cocoa powder, coconut sugar, baking powder, and salt together in a medium mixing bowl. Switch to a wooden spoon and stir in the melted chocolate, melted coconut oil, and honey. The batter will be thick. Add the eggs one at a time, stirring well after each addition. After you add the last egg, stir the batter until smooth. Spread the batter into the prepared pan.

Bake until a cake tester inserted in the center of the pan comes out clean, about 25 minutes.

Allow the brownies to cool in the pan. Remove the brownies from the pan using the parchment overhang and cut into squares.

. . . .

Wrap brownies in plastic wrap and store on the counter for up to 3 days, or freeze, wrapped in plastic wrap and placed in a freezer container, for up to 6 weeks.

. . . .

Chocolate Chip Cookie Bars

These chocolate chip cookie bars are cakey, studded with chocolate chips, and scented with vanilla. They are a wee bit easier to make than chocolate chip cookies. Instead of plopping mounds of dough on a baking sheet, you just spread batter into a pan and bake.

Active Time: 10 minutes
Bake Time: 25 minutes
Yield: 9 bars

57 grams (½ cup) coconut flour

½ teaspoon baking powder, homemade (page 210) or grain-free store-bought

¼ teaspoon salt

85 grams (¼ cup) honey

85 grams (¼ cup) unsulphured molasses

57 grams (¼ cup) coconut oil or unsalted butter, melted and cooled slightly

2 teaspoons vanilla extract

3 large eggs (about 150 grams out of the shell)

85 grams (½ cup) dairy-free dark chocolate chips or chunks

Adjust an oven rack to the middle position and preheat the oven to 350°F. Spray a 9-inch square cake pan with nonstick cooking spray. Cut a piece of parchment paper as wide as the pan and long enough to overhang the edges of the pan by 2 inches. Place the parchment in the pan. Run your finger along the edge of the parchment so it fits snuggly in the pan. Spray the parchment with nonstick cooking spray or brush with melted coconut oil.

Whisk the coconut flour, baking powder, and salt together in a medium mixing bowl. Add the honey, molasses, melted coconut oil, and vanilla. Switch to a wooden spoon and stir until smooth. The batter will be very stiff. Add the eggs. It's okay to add all three at one time. Stir the batter until smooth. Add the chocolate chips and stir until combined. Spread the batter evenly into the prepared pan.

Bake until golden brown. A cake tester inserted into the center should come out clean, about 25 minutes.

Allow to cool in the pan on a wire rack. When completely cool, lift out of the pan with the parchment overhang and cut into squares.

Store on the counter, wrapped in plastic wrap, for up to 3 days. Freeze cooled, cut bars for up to 1 month wrapped in plastic wrap and placed in a freezer container. Thaw at room temperature.

Variation

Maple-Walnut Bars: Replace the honey and molasses with 170 grams (½ cup) maple syrup, and stir 85 grams (¾ cup) chopped toasted walnuts into the batter along with the chocolate chips. Feel free to omit the chocolate chips if you want a pure maple-walnut experience.

The World's Easiest Blondies

egg-free; coconut-free

These bars were inspired by the World's Easiest Cookies (page 107). They are egg-free and come together in minutes.

Active Time: about 10 minutes
Bake Time: about 30 minutes
Yield: 12 small or 9 medium bars

170 grams (1 ½ cups) finely ground almond flour

57 grams (½ cup) tapioca starch

45 grams (¼ cup) evaporated cane juice or coconut sugar

1 teaspoon baking powder, homemade (page 210) or grain-free store-bought

½ teaspoon salt

85 grams (6 tablespoons) milk, dairy-free or traditional

2 tablespoons honey

Adjust an oven rack to the middle position and preheat the oven to 350°F. Spray a 9-inch square cake pan with nonstick cooking spray. Cut a piece of parchment paper as wide as the pan and long enough to overhang the edges of the pan by 2 inches. Place the parchment in the pan, running your finger along the edge so it fits snuggly. Spray the parchment with nonstick cooking spray or brush with melted coconut oil.

Whisk the almond flour, tapioca starch, evaporated cane juice, baking powder, and salt together in a medium mixing bowl. Add the milk and honey and stir with a wooden spoon until the batter is smooth. Spoon the batter into the prepared pan.

Bake until golden brown. A cake tester inserted into the center should come out clean, about 30 minutes.

Allow to cool in the pan on a wire rack. When completely cool, lift out of the pan with the parchment overhang and cut into 9 or 12 bars.

. . . .

Wrap the bars in plastic wrap and store on the counter for up to 3 days. Freeze cooled, cut bars for up to 1 month wrapped in plastic wrap and placed in a freezer container. Thaw at room temperature.

. . . .

Variation

Blondie Mix-Ins: Add up to ½ cup of dairy-free dark chocolate chips, chopped nuts, dried fruit, or a combination of all three.

Tart Lemon Bars

The first lemon bar I ever ate came from Rosie's Bakery in Cambridge, Massachusetts. I was in my twenties at the time and after one bite, I wondered why I'd never had one before. The tangy lemon topping and shortbread-like base are the perfect combination of sweet and tart. I think they taste better the day after they're made—if you can wait that long.

Active Time: about 15 minutes
Bake Time: about 30 minutes total
Yield: 12 small or 9 large bars

Base

170 grams (1 ½ cups) finely ground almond flour

2 tablespoons tapioca starch

½ teaspoon salt

1 large egg (about 50 grams out of the shell)

2 tablespoons honey

Topping

85 grams (½ cup) evaporated cane juice*

2 teaspoons coconut flour

Finely grated zest of 1 lemon (about 1 tablespoon)

2 large eggs (about 100 grams out of the shell)

1 large egg yolk (about 15 grams)

3 tablespoons freshly squeezed lemon juice

* For this recipe, evaporated cane juice works best in the topping. Coconut sugar and maple sugar overpower the fresh lemon flavor.

Preheat the oven to 350°F. Spray a 9-inch square cake pan with nonstick cooking spray. Cut a piece of parchment paper as wide as the pan and long enough to overhang the edges of the pan by 2 inches. Place the parchment in the pan, running your finger along the edge so it fits snuggly. Spray the parchment with nonstick cooking spray or brush with melted coconut oil.

Prepare the base: Whisk together the almond flour, tapioca starch, and salt. Add the egg and honey and stir with a wooden spoon. The dough will be thick.

Press the dough into the prepared pan with your fingers. If the dough sticks to your fingers, dust your hands lightly with tapioca starch. Prick the dough all over with a fork.

Bake until lightly golden brown, about 12 minutes.

Remove the pan from the oven, but leave the oven on. Allow the base to cool slightly.

Prepare the topping: Whisk together the evaporated cane juice, coconut flour, and lemon zest. Add the eggs and egg yolk and whisk until smooth. Whisk in the lemon juice. Pour over the cookie base.

Bake until topping is set, about 15 minutes.

Allow to cool in the pan. When cool, lift out of the pan with the parchment overhang and cut into 9 or 12 bars.

. . . .

These bars are best the day after they are baked. Wrap leftovers in plastic wrap and store on the counter for up to 3 days, or freeze cooled, cut bars for up to 1 month. Thaw at room temperature.

. . . .

Cakes

Almond-Flour Yellow Cake
Coconut-Flour Yellow Cake
Almond-Coconut Flour Yellow Cake
Almond-Flour Chocolate Cake
Coconut-Flour Chocolate Cake
Almond-Coconut Flour Chocolate Cake
Classic Spice Cake
Raid-the-Pantry Carrot Cake
Gingerbread Cake
Fresh Pineapple Upside Down Cake
Apple Surprise Cake
Can't Beet It Chocolate Cake
Beautiful Berry Shortcake
Maple-Bacon Cupcakes
Quadruple Chocolate Cupcakes
Whoopie Pies
Easy Peasy Shortcakes
Frostings
Vanilla Frosting• Chocolate Frosting • Maple Frosting

Whipped Coconut Cream

Almond-Coconut Flour Yellow Cake, page 134

How to Prepare a Cake Pan

Grain-free cakes love to stick to the pan. Here's how to prevent that.

- Trace your cake pan onto a piece of parchment paper. Cut out the shape. (Or use store-bought precut parchment rounds.)

- Grease the pan with nonstick cooking spray or brush lightly with melted coconut oil.

- Place the parchment paper piece in the bottom of the pan. (Turn it over so the pencil marks won't come in contact with the batter.)

- Lightly grease the parchment with nonstick cooking spray or brush with melted coconut oil.

How to Make Even Cupcakes

Fill muffin cups with a scoop, like an ice cream scoop. You want one that holds about ¼ cup of batter.

How to Check a Cake for Doneness

Insert a cake tester or toothpick in the center of the cake. Don't check near the edge of the pan; that bakes faster than the center. The cake tester should come out clean or with one or two damp crumbs.

You can also lightly touch the middle of the cake. It should feel like a firm, damp sponge, and spring back. If it feels wet and squishy, it isn't done yet.

How to Cool Cakes

Allow cakes and cupcakes to cool in the pan for a few minutes. (Specific times are included in the recipes.) After the cake cools slightly, turn it out onto a wire rack. Peel off the parchment paper from the bottom of the cake. This allows the steam to escape and prevents your cake from getting soggy.

A few of the cakes in this book should be cooled completely in the pan.

How to Frost a Cake

The most important thing when frosting a cake? Temperature. You want your cake completely cool, so your frosting doesn't melt, and you want your frosting at room temperature. It should spread easily. If you make your frosting in advance, allow it to come to room temperature for an hour or more before using.

For Single or Layer Cakes

Use a dry pastry brush to gently sweep away any excess crumbs that are clinging to the outside of the cake. Place a generous amount of frosting, about ¾ cup, in the center of the cooled cake. Use a metal frosting spatula to spread it out from the center to the edges. To prevent crumbs from getting in your frosting, don't let the spatula touch the cake; keep it on the frosting. For a layer cake, stack the second cake on top and repeat.

To frost the sides of the cake, place about three tablespoons of frosting on the top of your metal spatula and gently spread frosting on the sides of the cake. Repeat until the entire cake is iced. Be gentle to prevent crumbs from getting into your frosting.

For an extra smooth finish, dip your spatula into hot water. Quickly dry the spatula and run it on the top of the cake. Repeat for the sides. The warmth of the spatula melts the frosting just a little for a smooth finish.

For Cupcakes

Place a generous amount, about two tablespoons, of frosting in the center of the cupcake. Use a metal spatula to spread the frosting out to the edges.

How to Freeze a Cake

Cakes may be frozen uniced or iced. For uniced cakes, allow the cake to cool, then wrap well with plastic wrap and freeze. For iced cakes, place the entire cake in the freezer until frosting is firm, at least 6 hours or overnight. Remove the cake from the freezer, and working quickly so the frosting doesn't soften, wrap the cake well with plastic wrap, and then wrap with heavy-duty aluminum foil. Return the cake to the freezer. The maximum time you can store cakes in the freezer is included in the recipes.

If you don't have room in your freezer for an entire cake, cut it into slices and slide the pieces into plastic freezer bags. For iced pieces, place the slices on a baking sheet, freeze until frosting hardens, then transfer to freezer bags.

When ready to enjoy, remove the wrapped cake from the freezer and place on a platter. Allow to thaw for about three hours in the refrigerator, then remove the foil and plastic wrap and allow to thaw at room temperature for about four to six hours. You can also continue to thaw the unwrapped cake in the refrigerator; allow about eight hours (or overnight).

To thaw individual slices, remove them from the freezer bag. Place each slice on a plate and cover lightly with plastic wrap. Allow to thaw at room temperature, about three hours. You can also thaw the cake overnight in the refrigerator.

Single Layer? Double Layer? Triple Layer? What?

The recipes for yellow cake and chocolate cake both contain three size variations. Most of the time, I bake single-layer cakes because I don't need a big cake sitting in the kitchen. However, for birthdays or other celebrations, I bake multilayer cakes. I figure that you do the same.

When you want a single cake, select the single layer option. When you want a classic double-layer cake—the kind most traditional grain-filled boxed cake mixes make—bake two layers. And for those wonderful times in life when you want a mile-high cake, well then, the triple layer is for you!

If you are making a two- or three-layer cake or larger batch of cupcakes but only have one cake pan or 12-cup muffin pan, allow the cake or cupcakes to cool according to the recipe, then allow the pan to cool. Reline the pan and repeat with the remaining batter.

Almond-Flour Yellow Cake `coconut-free`

Yellow cake is a tried-and-true classic, perfect for birthdays or any celebration, big or small. If you're making a double or triple layer cake, fill the layers with your favorite frosting or jam. I'm partial to yellow cake filled with raspberry jam and iced with chocolate frosting.

Active Time: 10 to 15 minutes; plus about 30 minutes for frosting cakes
Bake Time: about 30 minutes
Yield: Single Layer: 1 (8-inch round) cake
Double Layer: 2 (8-inch round) cake layers
Triple Layer: 3 (8-inch round) cake layers

Single Layer

170 grams (1 ½ cups) finely ground almond flour

57 grams (½ cup) tapioca starch

85 grams (½ cup) coconut sugar or evaporated cane juice

1 teaspoon baking powder, homemade (page 210) or grain-free store-bought

½ teaspoon salt

66 grams (⅓ cup) grapeseed oil

3 large eggs (about 150 grams out of the shell)

57 grams (¼ cup) milk, dairy-free or traditional

1 teaspoon vanilla extract

2 cups Vanilla Frosting, Chocolate Frosting, or Maple Frosting (pages 168-169), optional

Double Layer

340 grams (3 cups) finely ground almond flour

113 grams (1 cup) tapioca starch

170 grams (1 cup) coconut sugar or evaporated cane juice

2 teaspoons baking powder, homemade (page 210) or grain-free store-bought

1 teaspoon salt

132 grams (⅔ cups) grapeseed oil

6 large eggs (about 300 grams out of the shell)

113 grams (½ cup) milk, dairy-free or traditional

2 teaspoons vanilla extract

4 cups Vanilla Frosting, Chocolate Frosting, or Maple Frosting (pages 168-169), optional

Triple Layer

510 grams (4 ½ cups) finely ground almond flour

170 grams (1 ½ cups) tapioca starch

255 grams (1 ½ cups) coconut sugar or evaporated cane juice

1 tablespoon baking powder, homemade (page 210) or grain-free store-bought

1 ¼ teaspoons salt

198 grams (1 cup) grapeseed oil

9 large eggs (about 450 grams out of the shell)

170 grams (¾ cup) milk, dairy-free or traditional

2 ½ teaspoons vanilla extract

6 cups Vanilla Frosting, Chocolate Frosting, or Maple Frosting (pages 168-169), optional

Adjust an oven rack to the middle position and preheat the oven to 350°F. Grease one, two, or three 8-inch round cake pans with nonstick cooking spray or brush lightly with melted coconut oil. Place an 8-inch parchment-paper round in the bottom of each pan and grease it lightly with nonstick cooking spray or brush lightly with melted coconut oil.

Whisk the almond flour, tapioca starch, coconut sugar, baking powder, and salt together in a medium mixing bowl for single or double layers, or a large mixing bowl for three layers. Add the oil, eggs, milk, and vanilla and whisk until smooth. (I suggest using a handheld mixer to mix the triple layer cake.)

Spread the batter evenly into the prepared cake pan(s). Gently tap the pan on the counter to settle the batter. Bake until a cake tester inserted in the center of each cake comes out clean, about 30 minutes. For the double and triple layer cakes, switch the position of the cake pans halfway through for even baking.

Allow the cake(s) to cool in the pan for about 8 minutes, then turn out to a wire rack to cool completely. Peel off the parchment paper.

Ice, if desired, with vanilla, chocolate, or maple frosting (see page 126).

. . . .

Store on the counter, covered, for up to 3 days. Freeze, wrapped in plastic wrap and then in heavy-duty foil, for up to 6 weeks. May be frozen iced or uniced. (For information on how to freeze cakes, see page 126.)

. . . .

BAKER'S NOTE: *Cupcakes*

It's easy to make this recipe into cupcakes! Here's how to do it:

Single Layer: makes 12 cupcakes
Double Layer: makes 24 cupcakes
Triple Layer: makes 36 cupcakes

Directions:

Line cupcake pans with paper liners. Prepare cake batter as directed. Fill each cupcake cup about two-thirds full. Bake until the cupcakes spring back to the touch, about 20 minutes per pan. A cake tester inserted into the center of a cupcake should come out clean or with a few dry crumbs clinging to it. Allow cupcakes to cool in the pan for five minutes and then transfer them to a wire rack to cool completely. If desired, frost with your favorite frosting when cupcakes are cool.

Coconut-Flour Yellow Cake `almond-free`

If you happen to have an open bag of chocolate chips around, try throwing a few into the batter. The idea comes from my mom who always finds ways to infuse a little joy into each day. She says whoever gets the slice with the chocolate chips is guaranteed a "lucky day." Cake and a lucky day? It doesn't get much better than that!

Active Time: 10 to 15 minutes; plus about 30 minutes for frosting cakes
Bake Time: about 30 minutes
Yield: Single Layer: 1 (8-inch round) cake
Double Layer: 2 (8-inch round) cake layers
Triple Layer: 3 (8-inch round) cake layers

Single Layer

57 grams (½ cup) coconut flour

1 teaspoon baking powder, homemade (page 210) or grain-free store-bought

½ teaspoon salt

75 grams (⅓ cup) coconut oil, melted and cooled slightly

4 large eggs (about 200 grams out of the shell)

113 grams (⅓ cup) honey

1 teaspoon vanilla extract

2 cups Vanilla Frosting, Chocolate Frosting, or Maple Frosting (pages 168-169), optional

Double Layer

113 grams (1 cup) coconut flour

2 teaspoons baking powder, homemade (page 210) or grain-free store-bought

1 teaspoon salt

150 grams (⅔ cup) coconut oil, melted and cooled slightly

8 large eggs (about 400 grams out of the shell)

226 grams (⅔ cup) honey

2 teaspoons vanilla extract

4 cups Vanilla Frosting, Chocolate Frosting, or Maple Frosting (pages 168-169), optional

Triple Layer

168 grams (1 ½ cups) coconut flour

1 tablespoon baking powder, homemade (page 210) or grain-free store-bought

1 ¼ teaspoons salt

225 grams (1 cup) coconut oil, melted and cooled slightly

12 large eggs (about 600 grams out of the shell)

340 grams (1 cup) honey

2 ½ teaspoons vanilla extract

6 cups Vanilla Frosting, Chocolate Frosting, or Maple Frosting (pages 168-169), optional

Adjust an oven rack to the middle position and preheat the oven to 350°F. Grease one, two, or three 8-inch round cake pans with nonstick cooking spray or brush lightly with melted coconut oil. Place an 8-inch parchment-paper round in the bottom of each pan and grease it lightly with nonstick cooking spray or brush lightly with melted coconut oil.

Whisk the coconut flour, baking powder, and salt together in a medium mixing bowl for single or double layers, or a large mixing bowl for three layers. Add the melted coconut oil, eggs, honey, and vanilla and whisk until smooth. (I suggest using a handheld mixer to mix the triple layer cake.) The batter will be thick.

Spoon the batter into the prepared pan(s). Smooth the batter with an angled metal spatula or the back of a spoon. Tap the pan(s) lightly on the counter to settle the batter. Bake until a cake tester inserted in the center of each cake comes out clean, about 30 minutes. For the double and triple layer cakes, switch the position of the pans halfway through for even baking.

Allow the cake(s) to cool in the pan for about 8 minutes, then turn out to a wire rack to cool completely.

Ice, if desired, with vanilla or chocolate frosting or maple buttercream (see page 126).

. . . .

Store on the counter, covered, for up to 3 days. Freeze, wrapped in plastic wrap and then in heavy-duty foil, for up to 6 weeks. May be frozen iced or uniced. (For information on how to freeze cakes, see page 126.)

. . . .

BAKER'S NOTE: *Cupcakes*

It's easy to make this recipe into cupcakes! Here's how to do it:

Single Layer: makes 12 cupcakes
Double Layer: makes 24 cupcakes
Triple Layer: makes 36 cupcakes

Directions:

Line cupcake pans with paper liners. Prepare cake batter as directed. Fill each cupcake cup about two-thirds full. Bake until the cupcakes spring back to the touch, about 20 minutes per pan. A cake tester inserted into the center of a cupcake should come out clean or with a few dry crumbs clinging to it. Allow cupcakes to cool in the pan for five minutes and then transfer them to a wire rack to cool completely. If desired, frost with your favorite frosting when cupcakes are cool.

Almond-Coconut Flour Yellow Cake

I know. I know. People hate the m-word: moist. But I really want to tell you that this cake is . . . moist. Its texture reminds me of a box cake mix but better. If you're making a double layer cake and want something a little different, why not make one layer of this yellow cake and one layer of chocolate cake? This way, you'll get the best of both worlds!

Active Time: 10 to 15 minutes; plus about 30 minutes for frosting cakes
Bake Time: about 30 minutes
Yield: Single Layer: 1 (8-inch round) cake
Double Layer: 2 (8-inch round) cake layers
Triple Layer: 3 (8-inch round) cake layers

Single Layer

113 grams (1 cup) finely ground almond flour

28 grams (¼ cup) coconut flour

85 grams (½ cup) coconut sugar

1 teaspoon baking powder, homemade (page 210) or grain-free store-bought

½ teaspoon salt

4 large eggs (about 200 grams out of the shell)

57 grams (¼ cup) milk, dairy-free or traditional

1 teaspoon vanilla extract

2 cups Vanilla Frosting, Chocolate Frosting, or Maple Frosting (pages 168-169), optional

Double Layer

227 grams (2 cups) finely ground almond flour

57 grams (½ cup) coconut flour

170 grams (1 cup) coconut sugar

2 teaspoons baking powder, homemade (page 210) or grain-free store-bought

1 teaspoon salt

8 large eggs (about 400 grams out of the shell)

113 grams (½ cup) milk, dairy-free or traditional

2 teaspoons vanilla extract

4 cups Vanilla Frosting, Chocolate Frosting, or Maple Frosting (pages 168-169), optional

Triple Layer

340 grams (1 cup) finely ground almond flour

85 grams (¾ cup) coconut flour

255 grams (1 ½ cups) coconut sugar

1 tablespoon baking powder, homemade (page 210) or grain-free store-bought

1 ¼ teaspoons salt

12 large eggs (about 600 grams out of the shell)

170 grams (¾ cup) milk, dairy-free or traditional

2 ½ teaspoons vanilla extract

6 cups Vanilla Frosting, Chocolate Frosting, or Maple Frosting (pages 168-169), optional

Adjust an oven rack to the middle position and preheat the oven to 350°F. Grease one, two, or three 8-inch round cake pans with nonstick cooking spray or brush lightly with melted coconut oil. Place an 8-inch parchment-paper round in the bottom of each pan and grease it lightly with nonstick cooking spray or brush lightly with melted coconut oil.

Whisk the almond flour, tapioca starch, coconut sugar, baking powder, and salt together in a medium mixing bowl for single or double layers, or a large mixing bowl for three layers. Add the oil, eggs, milk, and vanilla and whisk until smooth. (I suggest using a handheld mixer to mix the triple layer cake.) The batter will be thick.

Spread the batter evenly into the prepared cake pan(s). Gently tap pan on the counter to settle batter. Bake until a cake tester inserted in the center of the cake(s) comes out clean, about 30 minutes. For the double and triple layer cakes, switch the position of the pans halfway through for even baking.

Allow the cake(s) to cool in the pan for about 8 minutes, then turn out to a wire rack to cool completely. Peel off the parchment paper.

Ice, if desired, with vanilla, chocolate, or maple frosting (see page 126).

· ·

Store on the counter, covered, for up to 3 days. Freeze, wrapped in plastic wrap and then in heavy-duty foil, for up to 6 weeks. May be frozen iced or uniced. (For information on how to freeze cakes, see page 126.)

· ·

BAKER'S NOTE: *Cupcakes*

It's easy to make this recipe into cupcakes! Here's how to do it:

　　Single Layer: makes 12 cupcakes
　　Double Layer: makes 24 cupcakes
　　Triple Layer: makes 36 cupcakes

Directions:

Line cupcake pans with paper liners. Prepare cake batter as directed. Fill each cupcake cup about two-thirds full. Bake until the cupcakes spring back to the touch, about 20 minutes per pan. A cake tester inserted into the center of a cupcake should come out clean or with a few dry crumbs clinging to it. Allow cupcakes to cool in the pan for five minutes and then transfer them to a wire rack to cool completely. If desired, frost with your favorite frosting when cupcakes are cool.

Almond-Flour Chocolate Cake `coconut-free`

Chocolate cake magically turns any gathering into a celebration, and this cake is no exception. Rich and chocolatey, it tastes just like a chocolate cake should.

Active Time: 10 to 15 minutes; plus about 30 minutes for frosting cakes
Bake Time: about 30 minutes
Yield: Single Layer: 1 (8-inch round) cake
Double Layer: 2 (8-inch round) cake layers
Triple Layer: 3 (8-inch round) cake layers

Single Layer

170 grams (1 ½ cups) finely ground almond flour

50 grams (½ cup) natural cocoa powder

85 grams (½ cup) coconut sugar or evaporated cane juice

½ teaspoon baking soda

½ teaspoon salt

66 grams (⅓ cup) grapeseed oil

3 large eggs (about 150 grams out of the shell)

57 grams (¼ cup) milk, dairy-free or traditional

2 cups Vanilla Frosting, Chocolate Frosting, or Maple Frosting (pages 168-169), optional

Double Layer

340 grams (3 cups) finely ground almond flour

100 grams (1 cup) natural cocoa powder

170 grams (1 cup) coconut sugar or evaporated cane juice

1 teaspoon baking soda

1 teaspoon salt

132 grams (⅔ cup) grapeseed oil

6 large eggs (about 300 grams out of the shell)

113 grams (½ cup) milk, dairy-free or traditional

4 cups Vanilla Frosting, Chocolate Frosting, or Maple Frosting (pages 168-169), optional

Triple Layer

510 grams (4 ½ cups) finely ground almond flour

150 grams (1 ½ cups) natural cocoa powder

255 grams (1 ½ cups) coconut sugar or evaporated cane juice

1 ½ teaspoons baking soda

1 teaspoon salt

198 grams (1 cup) grapeseed oil

9 large eggs (about 450 grams out of the shell)

170 grams (¾ cup) milk, dairy-free or traditional

6 cups Vanilla Frosting, Chocolate Frosting, or Maple Frosting (pages 168-169), optional

Adjust an oven rack to the middle position and preheat the oven to 350°F. Grease one, two, or three 8-inch round cake pans with nonstick cooking spray or brush lightly with melted coconut oil. Place an 8-inch parchment-paper round in the bottom of each pan and grease it lightly with nonstick cooking spray or brush lightly with melted coconut oil.

Whisk the almond flour, cocoa powder, coconut sugar, baking soda, and salt together in a medium mixing bowl for single or double layers, or a large mixing bowl for three layers. Add the oil, eggs, and milk and whisk until smooth. (I suggest using a handheld mixer to mix the triple layer cake.)

Spread batter evenly into the prepared cake pan(s) with an angled metal spatula. Gently tap cake pan(s) on the counter to settle the batter. Bake until a cake tester inserted in the center of each cake comes out clean, about 30 minutes. For the double and triple layer cakes, switch the position of the pans halfway through for even baking.

Allow the cake(s) to cool in the pan for about 8 minutes, then turn out to a wire rack to cool completely. Peel off the parchment paper.

Ice, if desired, with vanilla, chocolate, or maple frosting (see page 126).

. . . .

Store on the counter, covered, for up to 3 days. Freeze, wrapped in plastic wrap and then in heavy-duty foil, for up to 6 weeks. May be frozen iced or uniced. (For information on how to freeze cakes, see page 126.)

. . . .

BAKER'S NOTE: *Cupcakes*

It's easy to make this recipe into cupcakes! Here's how to do it:

Single Layer: makes 12 cupcakes
Double Layer: makes 24 cupcakes
Triple Layer: makes 36 cupcakes

Directions:

Line cupcake pans with paper liners. Prepare cake batter as directed. Fill each cupcake cup about two-thirds full. Bake until the cupcake springs back to the touch, about 20 minutes per pan. A cake tester inserted into the center of the cupcake should come out clean or with a few dry crumbs clinging to it. Allow cupcakes to cool in the pan for five minutes and then transfer them to a wire rack to cool completely. If desired, frost with your favorite frosting when cupcakes are cool.

Coconut-Flour Chocolate Cake `almond-free`

This cake is light in texture with an intense chocolate flavor. It's great frosted or finished with whipped coconut cream or served as a single layer simply dusted with confectioner's sugar.

Active Time: 10 to 15 minutes; plus about 30 minutes for frosting cakes
Bake Time: about 30 minutes
Yield: Single Layer: 1 (8-inch round) cake
Double Layer: 2 (8-inch round) cake layers
Triple Layer: 3 (8-inch round) cake layers

Single Layer

50 grams (½ cup) natural cocoa powder

36 grams (⅓ cup) coconut flour

½ teaspoon baking soda

½ teaspoon salt

75 grams (⅓ cup) coconut oil, melted and cooled slightly

4 large eggs (about 200 grams out of the shell)

113 grams (⅓ cup) honey

2 cups Vanilla Frosting, Chocolate Frosting, or Maple Frosting (pages 168-169), optional

Double Layer

100 grams (1 cup) cup natural cocoa powder

74 grams (⅔ cup) coconut flour

1 teaspoon baking soda

1 teaspoon salt

150 grams (⅔ cup) coconut oil, melted and cooled slightly

8 large eggs (about 400 grams out of the shell)

226 grams (⅔ cup) honey

4 cups Vanilla Frosting, Chocolate Frosting, or Maple Frosting (pages 168-169), optional

Triple Layer

150 grams (1 ½ cups) natural cocoa powder

113 grams (1 cup) coconut flour

1 ½ teaspoons baking soda

1 ¼ teaspoons salt

225 grams (1 cup) coconut oil, melted and cooled slightly

12 large eggs (about 600 grams out of the shell)

340 grams (1 cup) honey

6 cups Vanilla Frosting, Chocolate Frosting, or Maple Frosting (pages 168-169), optional

Adjust an oven rack to the middle position and preheat the oven to 350°F. Grease one, two, or three 8-inch round cake pans with nonstick cooking spray or brush lightly with melted coconut oil. Place an 8-inch parchment-paper round in the bottom of each pan and grease it lightly with nonstick cooking spray or brush lightly with melted coconut oil.

Whisk the cocoa powder, coconut flour, baking soda, and salt together in a medium mixing bowl for single or double layers, or a large mixing bowl

for three layers. Add the melted coconut oil, eggs, and honey and whisk until smooth. (I suggest using a handheld mixer to mix the triple layer cake.) The batter will be thick.

Spoon the batter into the prepared pan(s). Smooth the batter with an angled metal spatula or the back of a spoon. Tap the pan(s) lightly on the counter to settle the batter. Bake until a cake tester inserted in the center of each cake comes out clean, about 30 minutes. For the double and triple layer cakes, switch the position of the pans halfway through for even baking.

Allow the cake(s) to cool in the pan for about 8 minutes, then turn out to a wire rack to cool completely.

Ice, if desired, with vanilla, chocolate, or maple frosting (see page 126).

. . . .

Store on the counter, covered, for up to 3 days. Freeze, wrapped in plastic wrap and then in heavy-duty foil, for up to 6 weeks. May be frozen iced or uniced. (For information on how to freeze cakes, see page 126.)

. . . .

BAKER'S NOTE: *Cupcakes*

It's easy to make this recipe into cupcakes! Here's how to do it:

    Single Layer: makes 12 cupcakes
    Double Layer: makes 24 cupcakes
    Triple Layer: makes 36 cupcakes

Directions:

Line cupcake pans with paper liners. Prepare cake batter as directed. Fill each cupcake cup about two-thirds full. Bake until the cupcakes spring back to the touch, about 20 minutes per pan. A cake tester inserted into the center of a cupcake should come out clean or with a few dry crumbs clinging to it. Allow cupcakes to cool in the pan for five minutes and then transfer them to a wire rack to cool completely. If desired, frost with your favorite frosting when cupcakes are cool.

Almond-Coconut Flour Chocolate Cake

This cake has a secret ingredient: coffee. It enhances the chocolate flavor without overpowering it or adding a mocha flavor. If you don't care for coffee, use water instead. Either way, this cake bakes up tender and full of flavor.

Active Time: 10 to 15 minutes; plus about 30 minutes for frosting cakes
Bake Time: about 30 minutes
Yield: Single Layer: 1 (8-inch round) cake
Double Layer: 2 (8-inch round) cake layers
Triple Layer: 3 (8-inch round) cake layers

Single Layer

57 grams (½ cup) finely ground almond flour

50 grams (½ cup) natural cocoa powder

36 grams (⅓ cup) coconut flour

1 teaspoon baking soda

¼ teaspoon salt

3 large eggs (about 150 grams out of the shell)

100 grams (⅓ cup) dark maple syrup

75 grams (⅓ cup) coconut oil or unsalted butter, melted and cooled slightly

113 grams (½ cup) full-fat coconut milk, whisked until smooth, or half-and-half

45 grams (3 tablespoons) cooled brewed coffee or water

2 cups Vanilla Frosting, Chocolate Frosting, or Maple Frosting (pages 168-169), optional

Double Layer

113 grams (1 cup) finely ground almond flour

100 grams (1 cup) natural cocoa powder

74 grams (⅔ cup) coconut flour

2 teaspoons baking soda

½ teaspoon salt

6 large eggs (about 300 grams out of the shell)

200 grams (⅔ cup) dark maple syrup

150 grams (⅔ cup) coconut oil or unsalted butter, melted and cooled slightly

226 grams (1 cup) full-fat coconut milk, whisked until smooth, or half-and-half

90 grams (6 tablespoons) cooled brewed coffee or water

4 cups Vanilla Frosting, Chocolate Frosting, or Maple Frosting (pages 168-169), optional

Triple Layer

170 grams (1 ½ cups) finely ground almond flour

150 grams (1 ½ cup) natural cocoa powder

113 grams (1 cup) coconut flour

1 tablespoon baking soda

¾ teaspoon salt

9 large eggs (about 450 grams out of the shell)

300 grams (1 cup) dark maple syrup

225 grams (1 cup) coconut oil or unsalted butter, melted and cooled slightly

1 (13.5-ounce) can full-fat coconut milk, whisked until smooth, or 377 grams (1 ⅔ cups) half-and-half

120 grams (½ cup) cooled brewed coffee or water

6 cups Vanilla Frosting, Chocolate Frosting, or Maple Frosting (pages 168-169), optional

Adjust an oven rack to the middle position and preheat the oven to 350°F. Grease one, two, or three 8-inch round cake pans with nonstick cooking spray or brush lightly with melted coconut oil.

Place an 8-inch parchment-paper round piece in the bottom of each pan and grease it lightly with nonstick cooking spray or brush lightly with melted coconut oil.

Whisk the almond flour, cocoa powder, coconut flour, baking soda, and salt together in a large mixing bowl. Add the eggs, maple syrup, melted coconut oil, coconut milk, and coffee and mix until smooth with a handheld mixer. The batter will be thick.

Spoon the batter into the prepared pan(s). Smooth the batter with an angled metal spatula or the back of a spoon. Tap the pan(s) lightly on the counter to settle the batter. Bake until a cake tester inserted in the center of each cake comes out clean, about 30 minutes. For the double and triple layer cakes, switch the position of the pans halfway through for even baking.

Allow the cake(s) to cool in the pan for about 8 minutes, then turn out to a wire rack to cool completely.

Ice, if desired, with vanilla, chocolate, or maple frosting (see page 126).

• •
Store on the counter, covered, for up to 3 days. Freeze, wrapped in plastic wrap and then in heavy-duty foil, for up to 6 weeks. May be frozen iced or uniced. (For information on how to freeze cakes, see page 126.)
• •

BAKER'S NOTE: *Cupcakes*

It's easy to make this recipe into cupcakes! Here's how to do it:

    Single Layer: makes 12 cupcakes
    Double Layer: makes 24 cupcakes
    Triple Layer: makes 36 cupcakes

Directions:

Line cupcake pans with paper liners. Prepare cake batter as directed. Fill each cupcake cup about two-thirds full. Bake until the cupcakes spring back to the touch, about 20 minutes per pan. A cake tester inserted into the center of a cupcake should come out clean or with a few dry crumbs clinging to it. Allow cupcakes to cool in the pan for five minutes and then transfer them to a wire rack to cool completely. If desired, frost with your favorite frosting when cupcakes are cool.

Classic Spice Cake `coconut-free`

This simple spice cake contains just a hint of molasses, which adds a nice coffee-caramel note. I like this cake iced with vanilla frosting, but it's also lovely on its own.

Active Time: about 15 minutes
Bake Time: about 30 minutes
Yield: 1 (8-inch round) cake

198 grams (1 ¾ cups) finely ground almond flour

28 grams (¼ cup) tapioca starch

½ teaspoon baking soda

1 teaspoon ground ginger

1 teaspoon ground cinnamon

½ teaspoon ground nutmeg

¼ teaspoon ground cloves

½ teaspoon salt

2 large eggs (about 100 grams out of the shell)

85 grams (¼ cup) honey

57 grams (¼ cup) milk, dairy-free or traditional

2 tablespoons unsulphured molasses

1 teaspoon vanilla extract

½ teaspoon white vinegar

Vanilla Frosting (page 168), optional

Adjust an oven rack to the middle position and preheat the oven to 350°F. Grease an 8-inch round cake pan with nonstick cooking spray or brush with melted coconut oil. Place an 8-inch parchment-paper round in the pan and grease it with nonstick cooking spray or brush lightly with melted coconut oil.

Whisk the almond flour, tapioca starch, baking soda, ginger, cinnamon, nutmeg, cloves, and salt together in a medium mixing bowl. Add the eggs, honey, milk, molasses, vanilla, and vinegar and whisk until smooth. Spread the batter evenly into the prepared pan.

Bake until set and golden brown, about 30 minutes. A cake tester inserted in the center of the cake should come out clean.

Allow the cake to cool in the pan on a wire rack for 5 minutes, then turn the cake out onto the rack to cool completely. Peel off the parchment paper.

If desired, ice with vanilla frosting (see page 126)

. . . .
Store on the counter, covered, for up to 3 days. Freeze, wrapped in plastic wrap and then in heavy-duty foil, for up to 6 weeks. May be frozen iced or uniced. (For information on how to freeze cakes, see page 126.)
. . . .

Raid-the-Pantry Carrot Cake

Of course you can bake a carrot cake any time of year, but for some reason, I tend to make it more in the winter. I guess my baker's math goes something like this:

Snow storm + I feel like cake + Oh! There are carrots in the refrigerator = I'll make carrot cake!

No matter what time of year you make this, you'll be rewarded with a spicy cake that no one will guess is grain-free.

Active Time: about 20 minutes
Bake Time: about 40 minutes
Yield: 1 (8-inch round) cake

198 grams (1 ¾ cups) finely ground almond flour

21 grams (3 tablespoons) coconut flour

2 teaspoons baking powder, homemade (page 210) or grain-free store-bought

2 teaspoons ground cinnamon

½ teaspoon ground nutmeg

⅛ teaspoon ground cloves

½ teaspoon salt

4 large eggs (about 200 grams out of the shell)

150 grams (½ cup) dark maple syrup

100 grams (1 cup) grated peeled carrots (about 3 medium carrots)

74 grams (½ cup) dark raisins (optional)

Vanilla Frosting (page 168), optional

Adjust an oven rack to the middle position and preheat the oven to 350°F. Grease an 8-inch round cake pan with nonstick cooking spray or brush with melted coconut oil. Place an 8-inch parchment-paper round in the pan and grease it with nonstick cooking spray or brush lightly with melted coconut oil.

Whisk the almond flour, coconut flour, baking powder, cinnamon, nutmeg, cloves, and salt together in a medium mixing bowl. Add the eggs and maple syrup and whisk until smooth. Switch to a rubber spatula or wooden spoon and stir in the carrots and raisins until incorporated. Spread the batter evenly into the prepared pan.

Bake until set and golden brown, about 40 minutes. A cake tester inserted in the center of the cake should come out clean.

Allow the cake to cool completely in the pan on a wire rack. Turn the cake out onto the rack and peel off the parchment paper.

If desired, ice with vanilla frosting (see page 126).

• •

Store on the counter, covered, for up to 3 days. Freeze, wrapped in plastic wrap and then in heavy-duty foil, for up to 6 weeks. May be frozen iced or uniced. (For information on how to freeze cakes, see page 126.)

• •

Gingerbread Cake `starch-free`

Delicate, soft, and spicy, this gingerbread cake almost begs to be enjoyed with a hot cup of coffee or tea while taking a break from the busyness of the winter season.

Active Time: 20 minutes
Bake Time: 25 minutes
Yield: 1 (8-inch square) cake

170 grams (1 ½ cups) finely ground almond flour

28 grams (¼ cup) coconut flour

1 tablespoon ground ginger

2 teaspoons ground cinnamon

2 teaspoons baking powder, homemade (page 210) or grain-free store-bought

½ teaspoon ground nutmeg

½ teaspoon salt

¼ teaspoon ground cloves

4 large eggs (about 200 grams out of the shell)

75 grams (¼ cup) dark maple syrup

85 grams (¼ cup) unsulphured molasses

Adjust an oven rack to the middle position and preheat the oven to 350°F. Spray an 8-inch square cake pan with nonstick cooking spray or brush with melted coconut oil. Place an 8-inch parchment-paper square in the pan and grease it with nonstick cooking spray or brush lightly with melted coconut oil.

Whisk the almond flour, coconut flour, ginger, cinnamon, baking powder, nutmeg, salt, and cloves together in a medium mixing bowl. Add the eggs, maple syrup, and molasses and whisk until smooth. The batter will be thick. Spoon the batter into the prepared pan. Smooth the top of the batter with a metal spatula or the back of a spoon.

Bake until the cake springs back to the touch, about 25 minutes.

Allow the cake to cool completely in the pan on a wire rack. Turn the cake out onto the rack and peel off the parchment paper.

- -
Store on the counter, covered, for up to 3 days. Freeze, wrapped in plastic wrap and then in heavy-duty foil, for up to 6 weeks. May be frozen iced or uniced. (For information on how to freeze cakes, see page 126.)
- -

Fresh Pineapple Upside Down Cake

coconut-free or almond-free, depending on the cake batter used

You know what makes pineapple upside down cake even better? A grain-free version. Seriously. Almond and coconut add a layer of flavor that I didn't even know this cake needed. I've always enjoyed pineapple upside down cake. Now I love it. A lot. Grain-free baking win!

Active Time: about 20 minutes
Bake Time: about 30 minutes
Yield: 1 (8-inch round) cake

3 tablespoons coconut oil, solid, or unsalted butter, softened

57 grams (⅓ cup) coconut sugar or evaporated cane juice

6 (¼-inch-thick) rings fresh pineapple or 6 well-drained canned pineapple rings, quartered

1 tablespoon dark rum (optional)

Batter for 1 Single Layer Almond-Flour Yellow Cake (page 129), Coconut-Flour Yellow Cake* (page 131), or Almond-Coconut Flour Yellow Cake (page 134), unbaked

* Coconut-flour cake batter can be hard to spread over the pineapple, and the pineapple pieces might move. It works but it does take a little finesse with a small angled spatula.

Adjust an oven rack to the middle position and preheat the oven to 350°F.

Melt the coconut oil in an 8-inch cast-iron skillet over medium heat. Sprinkle the coconut sugar over the oil and stir with a wooden spoon until it begins to bubble and melt. Turn the heat down to low. Arrange the pieces of pineapple evenly throughout the pan. Do this carefully as the oil can splatter and spurt as you add the pineapple to the pan.

If you are using fresh pineapple, cook over low heat until it is fork-tender, about 5 minutes. (Skip this step if you are using canned pineapple.) Be sure heat remains low to prevent the sugar from burning.

Stir the rum into the cake batter. Remove the skillet from the stovetop and pour the batter into pan. Spread the batter over the pineapple pieces. Don't worry if some of the pieces move around underneath.

Bake the cake until set and golden brown, about 30 minutes.

Allow the cake to cool in the pan for 10 minutes. Carefully turn the cake out onto a large plate. To do this, invert a large plate onto the skillet. Hold the plate firmly with one hand and use the handle of the skillet to turn the whole thing over. Be careful; the skillet will be hot, so use a pot holder or towel. Enjoy warm or cooled.

Store on the counter, wrapped, for up to 2 days.

Apple Surprise Cake

coconut-free or almond-free, depending on the cake batter used

A layer of sliced apples hides at the bottom of this cake. If only all of life's surprises were so sweet!

Active Time: about 30 minutes
Bake Time: about 25 minutes
Yield: 1 (8-inch round) cake

2 large Granny Smith apples,* peeled and cored

2 tablespoons coconut oil, solid, or unsalted butter, softened

45 grams (¼ cup) coconut sugar or evaporated cane juice

2 teaspoons ground cinnamon

Batter for 1 Single Layer Almond-Flour Yellow Cake (page 129), Coconut-Flour Yellow Cake (page 131), or Almond-Coconut Flour Yellow Cake (page 134), unbaked

* Tart apples work best in this recipe.

Adjust an oven rack to the middle position and preheat the oven to 350°F.

Slice one of the apples into ½-inch-thick slices. Melt the coconut oil over medium heat in an 8-inch cast-iron skillet. Stir in the coconut sugar. Cook until the sugar bubbles, about 1 minute. Add the apple slices and stir to coat with the coconut oil and coconut sugar. Use the back of a spoon to spread the apples into one layer. Turn the heat down to low and cook until the apples soften, about 5 minutes.

While the apples cook, dice the remaining apple into small bite-size pieces. Stir the diced apple and cinnamon into the batter. Spread the batter over the cooked apples.

Transfer the skillet to the oven and bake until golden brown, about 25 minutes. A cake tester inserted into the center of the cake should come out clean, about 25 minutes.

Allow the cake to cool in the pan. Carefully turn the cake out onto a large plate. To do this, invert a large plate onto the skillet. Hold the plate firmly with one hand and use the handle of the skillet to turn the whole thing over. Be careful; the skillet will be hot, so use a pot holder or towel.

Store in the refrigerator, wrapped, for up to 3 days. Allow to come to room temperature before serving.

Can't Beet It Chocolate Cake

almond-free; starch-free

I knew this cake recipe was a winner when my husband, an avowed beet-hater, loved it. The beets add a sweet-earthy note that isn't too vegetal, I promise. You can either steam fresh beets or buy them. Most grocery stores carry vacuum-packed steamed beets and they work great in this recipe.

Active Time: 15 minutes
Bake Time: about 30 minutes, plus about 15 minutes for steaming the beets
Yield: 1 (8-inch round) cake

227 grams (8 ounces, about 6 small) beets

57 grams (½ cup) coconut flour

2 tablespoons cocoa powder, natural or Dutch-process

1 teaspoon baking soda

½ teaspoon salt

75 grams (⅓ cup) coconut oil or unsalted butter, melted and cooled slightly

113 grams (⅓ cup) honey

2 tablespoons white vinegar

4 large eggs (about 200 grams out of the shell)

Vanilla Frosting (page 168), optional

Lightly scrub the beets. Trim the stems and ends and quarter them. Leave the skin intact. Pour about 1 inch water into a pot. Place the beets in a steamer basket over the water. Cover the pot and steam them until tender, about 15 minutes (larger beets will take longer). The beets should give easily when pierced with a fork. Allow to cool.

Meanwhile, adjust an oven rack to the middle position and preheat the oven to 350°F. Grease an 8-inch round cake pan with nonstick cooking spray or melted coconut oil. Place an 8-inch parchment-paper round in the pan and grease it with nonstick cooking spray or brush lightly with melted coconut oil.

Use a paring knife to remove the skin from the beets. Place the beets in a food processor or high-powered blender and blend until almost smooth. It's fine if some small chunks remain.

Whisk the coconut flour, cocoa powder, baking soda, and salt together in a medium mixing bowl. Add the melted coconut oil, honey, and vinegar and whisk until smooth. Add the beets and whisk until smooth. Add the eggs one at a time, whisking well after each addition. After you add the last egg, whisk for 15 seconds. The batter will be very thick. Spoon the batter into the prepared pan. Use a small offset spatula or the back of a small spoon to spread the batter evenly in the pan.

Bake until set, about 30 minutes. A cake tester inserted into the center of the cake should come out clean.

Allow the cake to cool in the pan for 5 minutes, then turn the cake out onto a wire rack to cool completely. Peel off the parchment paper.

If desired, ice with vanilla frosting (see page 126).

Store on the counter, covered, for up to 3 days. Freeze, wrapped in plastic wrap and then in heavy-duty foil, for up to 6 weeks. May be frozen iced or uniced. (For information on how to freeze cakes, see page 126.)

Beautiful Berry Shortcake

All berries are beautiful. But . . . some are a little beat up. I'm not talking about moldy berries. Avoid those. I'm talking about the ones that some farmers call "jam berries." They're a little bruised, or maybe a day or two past their peak. This isn't a bad thing. These berries make a fabulous—and budget-friendly—shortcake. If you ever see them, buy a pint. Macerate them with a little maple syrup or sugar and pile them on top of this cake.

Active Time: 30 minutes
Bake Time: 20 minutes
Yield: 1 (8-inch round) shortcake

Cake

113 grams (1 cup) finely ground almond flour

36 grams (⅓ cup) coconut flour

28 grams (¼ cup) tapioca starch

2 teaspoons baking powder, homemade (page 210) or grain-free store-bought

½ teaspoon salt

3 large eggs (about 150 grams out of the shell)

100 grams (⅓ cup) dark maple syrup

Topping

2 cups Whipped Coconut Cream (page 170) or whipped heavy cream

1 pint fresh berries (use whatever is in season) or Macerated Berries (see Variations)

Adjust an oven rack to the middle position and preheat the oven to 350°F. Grease an 8-inch round cake pan with nonstick cooking spray or brush lightly with melted coconut oil. Place an 8-inch parchment-paper round in the pan and grease it with nonstick cooking spray or brush lightly with melted coconut oil.

Whisk the almond flour, coconut flour, tapioca starch, baking powder, and salt together in a medium mixing bowl. Add the eggs and maple syrup and whisk until smooth. Spread the batter into the prepared cake pan.

Bake until brown and the top springs back to the touch, about 20 minutes.

Allow cake to cool in the pan for 5 minutes, then turn the cake out onto a wire rack to cool completely. Peel off the parchment paper.

When cool, ice with Whipped Coconut Cream (page 126) and top with berries.

. . . .
Store the cake in the refrigerator, covered, for up to 2 days.
. . . .

Variations

Berry-Free Shortcake: As much as I love a berry shortcake, I also love peach shortcake, plum shortcake, and, in the winter, pineapple shortcake. To make these variations, cut the fruit into bite-size pieces, or just slice the peaches and plums, if you prefer how that looks. Stir the fruit together with a little maple syrup and a teaspoon of vanilla extract. Allow to stand until a little bit of juice runs from the fruit, then spoon the fruit and the juice it yielded onto the cooled cake. Serve with whipped coconut cream or whipped cream, if desired.

Macerated Berries: Wash and drain 2 pints fresh berries. Cut into bite-size pieces if needed. (I only cut up large strawberries.) Place the berries in a large mixing bowl. Use the back of a fork to break up the berries. Stir in a little maple syrup or coconut sugar—start with 1 tablespoon and go from there, depending on the sweetness of the berries—and 1 teaspoon vanilla extract. Let stand until some juice runs from the berries, about 15 minutes.

Maple-Bacon Cupcakes `coconut-free`

These cupcakes were inspired by peanut butter and bacon sandwiches. Using almond butter instead of almond flour gives you a tender and easy-to-make sweet treat.

Active Time: 20 minutes
Bake Time: 20 minutes
Yield: 12 cupcakes

Cupcakes

285 grams (1 cup) almond butter, homemade (page 210) or store-bought

2 medium bananas, peeled and mashed (250 grams / ½ cup)

2 large eggs (about 100 grams out of the shell)

75 grams (¼ cup) dark maple syrup

1 teaspoon vanilla extract

1 teaspoon baking powder, homemade (page 210) or grain-free store-bought

2 strips bacon, cooked until crisp, drained, and crumbled

Topping

Maple Frosting (page 168)

2 strips bacon, cooked until crisp, drained, and crumbled

Adjust an oven rack to the middle position and preheat the oven to 350°F. Line 12 standard-size muffin cups with paper liners.

Combine almond butter, mashed banana, eggs, maple syrup, vanilla, and baking powder in a large bowl. Whisk until smooth. Stir in the bacon. Scoop the batter into the prepared muffin cups, filling each cup about two-thirds full.

Bake until the cupcakes spring back to the touch, about 18 minutes.

Allow cupcakes to cool in the pan for 5 minutes, then transfer them to a wire rack to cool completely.

When the cupcakes are cool, ice with maple frosting (see page 126) and top with the bacon.

Store on the counter, covered, for up to 3 days. Freezing is not recommended for these cupcakes because it adversely affects the texture of the bacon.

Quadruple Chocolate Cupcakes

almond-free; starch-free

What's better than chocolate? More chocolate, of course! In this recipe, the cocoa-y cupcakes and rich frosting are both studded with chocolate chips. And to finish, more chocolate chips are sprinkled on top. Make these for those times when chocolate feels like a requirement, not an option.

Active Time: 15 minutes
Bake Time: about 20 minutes
Yield: 9 cupcakes

Cupcakes

36 grams (⅓ cup) natural cocoa powder

36 grams (⅓ cup) coconut flour

½ teaspoon baking soda

½ teaspoon salt

170 grams (½ cup) honey

57 grams (¼ cup) coconut oil, melted and cooled slightly

4 large eggs (about 200 grams out of the shell)

78 grams (½ cup) dairy-free dark chocolate chips

Frosting

78 grams (½ cup) mini chocolate chips

1 cup Chocolate Frosting (page 169)

Adjust an oven rack to the middle position and preheat the oven to 350°F. Line 9 standard-size muffin cups with paper liners.

Whisk the cocoa powder, coconut flour, baking soda, and salt together in a medium mixing bowl. Add the honey and melted coconut oil and whisk until smooth. The batter will be thick. One at a time, whisk in the eggs. Be sure each egg is thoroughly incorporated before adding the next. Allow the batter to rest for 5 minutes.

Stir in the chocolate chips. Divide evenly between the prepared muffin cups. Each cup should be about two-thirds full. Lightly tap the pan on the counter. (This helps the batter settle evenly in the pan.)

Bake until the cupcakes are set and spring back to the touch, about 20 minutes.

Allow the cupcakes to cool in the pan for about 5 minutes, then transfer them to a wire rack to cool completely.

Stir about half of the mini chocolate chips into the frosting and ice the cupcakes (see page 126). Sprinkle the remaining chocolate chips on top.

. . . .

Store on the counter, covered, for up to 3 days. Freeze, wrapped in plastic wrap and then in heavy-duty foil, for up to 6 weeks. May be frozen iced or uniced. (For information on how to freeze cakes, see page 126.)

. . . .

Whoopie Pies

Whoopie pies are something of a riddle. They are both a cake and cookie, but not a pie. For a moment, they were heralded as the "new cupcake." Eh—to those of us from New England, whoopie pies aren't a new treat. They are old friends that you can find everywhere from corner gas stations to upscale bakeries (especially in Maine). The flavors vary from pumpkin to red velvet. I prefer the classic chocolate cake sandwiched together with a light, fluffy filling.

Active Time: about 1 hour
Bake Time: about 20 minutes
Yield: 6 large whoopie pies or 12 mini whoopie pies

Cakes

57 grams (½ cup) finely ground almond flour

36 grams (⅓ cup) coconut flour

25 grams (¼ cup) Dutch-process cocoa powder

1 teaspoon baking soda

½ teaspoon salt

75 grams (⅓ cup) coconut oil, solid, or unsalted butter, softened

85 grams (½ cup) coconut sugar or evaporated cane juice

2 large eggs (about 100 grams out of the shell)

85 grams (6 tablespoons) milk, dairy-free or traditional

Filling

113 grams (½ cup) palm shortening, solid, or unsalted butter, softened

226 grams (2 cups) powdered sugar, homemade (page 210) or grain-free store-bought

57 grams (¼ cup) milk, dairy-free or traditional

½ teaspoon vanilla extract

Adjust an oven rack to the middle position and preheat the oven to 350°F. Line a rimmed baking sheet with parchment paper.

Whisk the almond flour, coconut flour, cocoa powder, baking soda, and salt together in a medium mixing bowl. Beat together the coconut oil and coconut sugar in a second medium mixing bowl with a handheld mixer on medium speed until thick. If there are any large lumps of coconut oil, stop the mixer and squeeze the paste together with your hand, or break up the large lumps with a fork.

With the mixer running, add the eggs one at a time and mix until combined. Scrape down the sides of the bowl with a rubber spatula. Add the dry ingredients and mix until combined. The batter will be stiff.

Add the milk and mix until smooth. The batter will be thick.

Spoon about 1/4 cup batter for each cake (or 2 tablespoons for mini cakes) onto the prepared baking sheet, about 3 inches apart.

Bake until cakes spring back to the touch and are aromatic, about 20 minutes for large cakes and 14 minutes for mini ones.

Allow the cakes to cool on the pan for 5 minutes, then transfer them to a wire rack to cool completely.

While the cakes are cooling, make the filling: Combine the palm shortening, powdered sugar, milk, and vanilla in a large mixing bowl. Beat with a handheld mixer on medium speed until smooth.

When the cakes are cool, spread a generous amount (about two tablespoons for the large cakes and two teaspoons for the mini cakes) of filling over one of the cakes. Make a sandwich by pressing another cake on top. Repeat with remaining whoopie pies.

Store filled whoopie pies on the counter, covered, for up to 3 days or freeze, in a freezer container or bag, for up to 6 weeks.

Easy Peasy Shortcakes `almond-free`

For a fancy-pants dessert that's insanely easy to make, bake a batch of these shortcakes and serve them with vanilla-scented whipped coconut cream (page 170) and lots of fresh berries. But they aren't just for dessert—try one in the morning, split and spread with jam.

Active Time: 20 minutes
Bake Time: 20 minutes per pan
Yield: 12 shortcakes

113 grams (1 cup) coconut flour

85 grams (¾ cup) tapioca starch

1 ½ teaspoons baking powder, homemade (page 210) or grain-free store-bought

¾ teaspoon salt

85 grams (6 tablespoons) coconut oil, solid, or unsalted butter, softened

100 grams (⅔ cup) coconut sugar or evaporated cane juice

2 large eggs (about 100 grams out of the shell)

226 grams (1 cup) coconut milk, full-fat or reduced-fat

1 teaspoon vanilla extract

Adjust an oven rack to the middle position and preheat the oven to 350°F. Line a rimmed baking sheet with parchment paper.

Whisk the coconut flour, tapioca starch, baking powder, and salt together in a small mixing bowl.

Combine the coconut oil and coconut sugar in a large mixing bowl. Beat until smooth with a handheld mixer on medium-speed. If there are any large lumps of coconut oil in the mixture, stop the mixer and squeeze the paste together with your hand, or break up the large lumps with a fork.

Turn the mixer speed down to low and add the eggs one at a time. Be sure each egg incorporates before you add the next one.

Stop the mixer and scrape the bottom and sides of the bowl with a rubber spatula. Add half the dry ingredients. Turn the mixer to medium speed and beat until combined. In a slow and steady stream, add half the coconut milk and all of the vanilla. Stop the mixer and add the remaining dry ingredients. Beat on medium speed until smooth. In a slow and steady stream, add the remaining coconut milk. Mix until smooth.

Scoop about ¼ cup batter for each cake onto the prepared baking sheet, about three inches apart.

Bake until set and golden brown, about 20 minutes.

Allow the cakes to cool on the pan on a wire rack for 5 minutes, then transfer them to the rack to cool completely.

• •

Shortcakes are best enjoyed the day they are baked. Freeze leftovers in a freezer container or bag for up to 3 weeks.

• •

Frostings

Be sure to select sustainable palm shortening (see page 20 for more information). If you aren't comfortable using palm shortening and your diet includes dairy, replace it with unsalted butter. I don't recommend using coconut oil in frosting because it melts in a warm room (above 76°F).

Maple Frosting

almond-free; egg-free; coconut-free

Active Time: 10 minutes
Yield: about 2 cups

113 grams (½ cup) leaf lard or palm shortening, solid, or unsalted butter, softened

226 grams (2 cups) powdered sugar, homemade (page 210) or grain-free store-bought

3 tablespoons dark maple syrup

½ teaspoon salt

Combine the lard, powdered sugar, maple syrup, and salt in a large mixing bowl. Use a handheld mixer on medium speed to beat until smooth.

· ·

Use the frosting right away or store in the refrigerator, covered, for up to 3 days. Allow the frosting to come to room temperature, then rewhip before using.

· ·

Vanilla Frosting

almond-free; egg-free; coconut-free

Active Time: 10 minutes
Yield: 1 cup; enough for 1 (8-inch) cake or 12 cupcakes

226 grams (2 cups) powdered sugar, homemade (page 210) or grain-free store-bought

¼ teaspoon salt

113 grams (½ cup) palm shortening, solid, or unsalted butter, softened

57 grams (¼ cup) milk, dairy-free or traditional

½ teaspoon vanilla extract

Whisk the powdered sugar and salt together in a medium mixing bowl. Add the palm shortening and mix with a handheld mixer on medium speed until combined. Frosting will look dry. With the mixer running, add the milk in a slow and steady stream. Add the vanilla and mix until fluffy. If the frosting is too thick to spread, add an additional teaspoon or two of milk.

· ·

Use the frosting right away or store in the refrigerator, covered, for up to 5 days. Allow the frosting to come to room temperature, then rewhip before using.

· ·

Chocolate Frosting

almond-free; egg-free; coconut-free

Active Time: 10 minutes
Yield: 1 cup; enough for 1 (8-inch) cake or 12 cupcakes

226 grams (2 cups) powdered sugar, homemade (page 210) or grain-free store-bought

75 grams (3/4 cup) Dutch-process cocoa powder

¼ teaspoon salt

113 grams (½ cup) palm shortening, solid, or unsalted butter, softened

57 grams (¼ cup) milk, dairy-free or traditional

½ teaspoon vanilla extract

Whisk the powdered sugar, cocoa powder, and salt together in a medium mixing bowl. Add the palm shortening and mix with a handheld mixer on medium speed until combined. Frosting will be thick. With the mixer running, add the milk in a slow and steady stream. Add the vanilla and mix until fluffy. If the frosting is too thick to spread, add an additional teaspoon or two of milk.

· ·

Use the frosting right away or store in the refrigerator, covered, for up to 5 days. Allow the frosting to come to room temperature, then rewhip before using.

· ·

Variation

Super Chocolate Frosting: Prepare the chocolate frosting as directed. Melt and cool 85 grams (3 ounces) dark chocolate (72% cacao recommended); see Baker's Note on page 190. In a slow and steady stream, add the chocolate to the frosting while mixing. Chill the frosting for an hour, until firm but spreadable. Rewhip until fluffy just before using.

Whipped Coconut Cream   `almond-free; egg-free`

Whipped coconut cream was one of those "easy" recipes that tripped me up. Lots of people talked about how easy it was to whip the hard cream from the top of cans of coconut milk. Each time I tried, though, I ended up with a watery mess. Here's what I learned: some brands whip well, others don't. Coconut milk that contains gum (usually guar gum) often won't work. Although to confuse things further, sometimes they do. I know, crazy-making, right?

  I use Aroy D or Golden Star brand coconut milk. However, things change. You might need to try a few brands to see which whips up the best.

Active Time: 10 minutes
Chill Time: overnight
Yield: about 2 cups

2 (13.5-ounce) cans full-fat coconut milk

28 grams (¼ cup) powdered sugar, homemade (page 210) or grain-free store-bought

1 teaspoon vanilla extract

Place the cans of coconut milk in the refrigerator to chill overnight.

Open the cans and scoop the hardened coconut cream into a small mixing bowl. (If after an overnight chill, there isn't a layer of hard coconut cream, you can't make whipped cream with that brand.) Reserve leftover coconut milk for drinking or adding to smoothies. You don't need it for the whipped cream.

Use a handheld mixer on high speed to whip the cream until light and fluffy. (Sometimes it looks a little gray. This is normal.) In a slow and steady stream, pour in the powdered sugar and vanilla. Whip until combined. Serve.

. . . .
Store whipped coconut cream in a covered bowl in the refrigerator. Rewhip before serving.
. . . .

Essential Pies

Classic Double-Crust or Crumb-Topped Fruit Pie

Thanksgiving Pumpkin Pie

Sweet Potato Pie

The World's Easiest (and Richest!) Chocolate Pie

Flaky Pie Crust

Cookie Crumb Crust

Classic Double-Crust Apple Pie, page 174

Classic Double-Crust or Crumb-Topped Fruit Pie

I won't lie: working with grain-free double-crust pie dough takes a little finesse. The top crust sometimes doesn't want to play nice. Since the dough doesn't contain elastic gluten, once it falls into place it's hard to move, and it might break if you try.

If this sounds like more futzing than you feel like, follow the recipe for a crumb-topped pie. You get the flavor of a classic fruit pie without the hassle of working with a top crust.

Use a standard pie plate, not a deep-dish one. Grain-free crust tends to break apart as you try to fit it into the pan and doesn't take kindly to being baked in a deep pan.

Active Time: about 1 hour
Bake Time: about 45 minutes
Yield: 1 (9-inch) pie

1 Double Crust Flaky Pie Crust (page 182) or
   1 Single Crust (for a crumb-topped pie)

Apple, Blueberry, Peach, or Sour
   Cherry Filling (recipes follow)

Tapioca starch, for rolling the top crust (optional)

Crumb Topping (optional)

28 grams (¼ cup) finely ground almond flour

2 tablespoons evaporated cane juice or
   coconut sugar

2 teaspoons tapioca starch

28 grams (2 tablespoons) coconut oil, solid, or
   unsalted butter, softened

Adjust an oven rack to the middle position and preheat the oven to 425°F.

Remove the pie plate with the bottom pie crust from the refrigerator. Remove the plastic wrap. Spoon the fruit filling into the crust.

For a double-crust pie: Allow the dough for the top crust to come to room temperature. Place a 12 by 16-inch piece of parchment paper on the counter. Dust the parchment lightly with tapioca starch. Center the dough in the middle of the parchment and dust the top with tapioca starch. Cover with a second piece of parchment. Roll out the dough to a 12-inch circle between two pieces of parchment. Carefully pull away the top piece of parchment from the dough. Place the filled pie next to the top crust. Slide your hand under the bottom parchment. Lift the top crust off the counter and flip it onto the pie. Before you do this, eye things up. You want the top crust to land centered over the pie. Carefully peel away the parchment.

Trim the overhang, then crimp the edges together with a fork. Use a sharp knife to cut several slits in the top crust.

For a crumb-topped pie: Combine the almond flour, evaporated cane juice, and tapioca starch in a small bowl. Add the coconut oil and mix with a fork, pressing the mixture together until a paste forms. Use your fingertips to sprinkle small clumps of crumb topping all over the filling.

Place the pie on a rimmed baking sheet. Bake for 15 minutes, then turn the oven temperature down to 375°F. Bake until the filling bubbles and the crust turns golden brown, about 45 minutes for a double crust pie; 25 minutes for a crumb-topped pie.

Allow the pie to cool on a wire rack.

- -
Pie is best served the day it's made. Store leftover pie in the refrigerator, wrapped, for up to 3 days.
- -

Apple Filling

57 grams (⅓ cup) evaporated cane juice or coconut sugar

2 tablespoons tapioca starch

4 pounds apples, peeled, cored, and sliced (about 6 cups)

2 teaspoons freshly squeezed lemon juice

1 teaspoon ground cinnamon

¼ teaspoon salt

⅛ teaspoon ground nutmeg

Stir the evaporated cane juice and tapioca starch together in a large mixing bowl. Add the remaining ingredients and stir to combine.

Blueberry Filling

57 grams (⅓ cup) evaporated cane juice

28 grams (¼ cup) tapioca starch

2 ½ pints blueberries (5 cups), washed and stemmed

2 teaspoons finely grated lemon zest

2 tablespoons freshly squeezed lemon juice

Stir the evaporated cane juice and tapioca starch together in a large mixing bowl. Add the remaining ingredients and stir to combine.

Peach Filling

57 grams (⅓ cup) evaporated cane juice

3 tablespoons tapioca starch

2 ¾ pounds (about 8 medium) ripe peaches, peeled (see Baker's Note), pitted, and sliced

1 tablespoon freshly squeezed lemon juice

Stir the evaporated cane juice and tapioca starch together in a large mixing bowl. Add the remaining ingredients and stir to combine

BAKER'S NOTE: *How to Peel Peaches*

Fill a large bowl about halfway with cold water. Add a generous amount of ice (about 4 cups).

Bring a large pot of water to a boil.

Place peaches in the boiling water for about 15 seconds. Use a timer. You don't want to cook the peaches.

Remove the peaches from the boiling water with a slotted spoon and place immediately in the ice bath. Allow the peaches to cool.

Remove peaches from the ice water.

Use a paring knife to peel the skin off the peaches.

Sour Cherry Filling

85 grams (½ cup) evaporated cane juice

38 grams (⅓ cup) tapioca starch

2 pounds sour cherries,* pitted (about 5 cups)

½ teaspoon vanilla extract

* If you use Bing cherries, reduce the sugar to 57 grams (⅓ cup).

Stir the evaporated cane juice and tapioca starch together in a large mixing bowl. Add the remaining ingredients and stir to combine.

28 grams (2 tablespoons) coconut oil

Thanksgiving Pumpkin Pie

Baking the crust slightly before adding the filling ensures that the crust remains crisp and does not get soggy. I use store-bought pumpkin for my pie, but if you want to roast your own pumpkin or squash, check out the Baker's Note.

Active Time: 15 minutes if using canned pumpkin
Bake Time: about 50 minutes total
Yield: 1 (9-inch) pie

Single Crust Flaky Pie Crust (page 182)

1 (15-ounce) can pure pumpkin (not pumpkin pie filling)

226 grams (1 cup) full-fat coconut milk, whisked until smooth

2 large eggs (about 100 grams out of the shell)

85 grams (½ cup) coconut sugar, granulated maple sugar, or evaporated cane juice

2 teaspoons pumpkin pie spice, homemade (page 54) or store-bought

1 teaspoon vanilla extract

Whipped Coconut Cream (page 170), for serving (optional)

BAKER'S NOTE: *When is pumpkin not pumpkin?*

When it comes in a can. While the label may read "100% pure pumpkin," the reality is that most of the time manufacturers use a mix of squashes, like butternut, golden delicious, and Hubbard, or a pumpkin variety that's been bred over the years and now resembles a squash.

What does this mean for a baker? It means that if you want to make a homemade "pumpkin" pie, you should instead reach for butternut squash. It makes a much better filling.

To roast a butternut squash: Preheat the oven to 375°F. Cut a 3-pound squash in half lengthwise, scoop out and discard the seeds and fibers, and place the halves flesh side up on a rimmed baking sheet. Roast until tender, about 25 minutes. Remove the squash from the oven and allow to cool. Scoop the flesh out of the skin and puree in a food processor or food mill. Pour the pureed squash into a large piece of cheesecloth. Tie the corners of the cheesecloth, forming a makeshift bag. Hang the bag over a bowl and allow excess moisture to drip out for about 2 hours. Use the drained puree in place of the pumpkin called for in the recipe.

Adjust an oven rack to the middle position and preheat the oven to 350°F.

Place the pie plate with the crust on a rimmed baking sheet. Remove the plastic wrap and pierce the dough several times with a fork. Bake the crust until just barely brown, about 12 minutes.

Remove the crust from the oven but leave the oven on. Set aside the crust to cool while you make the filling.

Whisk the pumpkin, coconut milk, eggs, coconut sugar, pumpkin pie spice, and vanilla together until smooth. Spoon the filling into the crust.

Return the pie to the oven and bake until edges of the crust turn golden brown and filling sets around the edges and the center jiggles slightly, about 40 minutes.

Allow the pie to cool completely, then chill, uncovered, for 2 hours before serving.

Serve with whipped coconut cream, if desired.

Store leftover pie in the refrigerator, wrapped, for up to 3 days.

Sweet Potato Pie

This creamy sweet potato pie tastes a little more delicate to me than pumpkin pie. Be sure to try the variation made with a gingersnap crust. It's one of my favorite versions!

Active Time: 15 minutes
Bake Time: about 40 minutes for the sweet potatoes, about 1 hour 15 minutes for the pie
Yield: 1 (9-inch) pie

About 2 pounds (3 large) sweet potatoes

1 Single Crust Flaky Pie Crust (page 182)

4 large eggs (about 200 grams out of the shell)

226 grams (1 cup) full-fat coconut milk, whisked until smooth, or heavy cream

57 grams (⅓ cup) evaporated cane juice or coconut sugar

2 teaspoons ground cinnamon

½ teaspoon ground nutmeg

½ teaspoon salt

Whipped Coconut Cream (page 170), for serving (optional)

Adjust an oven rack to the middle position and preheat the oven to 350°F.

Wash the sweet potatoes. Pierce each a few times with a sharp knife. Place them on a rimmed baking sheet. Roast until tender, about 40 minutes. A knife inserted in the center of each should meet no resistance. Remove the sweet potatoes from the oven (leave the oven on) and set them aside to cool until you can handle them.

Place the pie plate with the crust on a rimmed baking sheet. Remove the plastic wrap and pierce the dough several times with a fork. Bake the crust until lightly golden brown, about 15 minutes. Remove the baking sheet with the pie plate from the oven but leave the oven on.

Remove and discard the skins from the sweet potatoes. Place the sweet potatoes in a large mixing bowl and mash with a fork until smooth. Add the eggs, coconut milk, evaporated cane juice, cinnamon, nutmeg, and salt and whisk to combine.

Spread the filling into the pie crust. Return the pie to the oven and bake until the edges are set and the center jiggles a little, about 1 hour.

Allow the pie to cool slightly before serving. Serve with whipped coconut cream, if desired.

Store leftover pie in the refrigerator, wrapped, for up to 3 days.

Variation

Sweet Potato Pie with Gingersnap Crust: Prepare and bake the cookie crumb crust on page 185 using gingersnaps. Prepare the pie filling and pour it into the crust. Bake and cool the pie as directed.

The World's Easiest (and Richest!) Chocolate Pie

Want a knockout dessert that's ridiculously easy to make? Then this pie is for you. And if you don't care about time and want the richest chocolate pie you've ever tasted, well, this recipe's for you, too!

Active Time: 10 minutes
Chill Time: at least 4 hours
Yield: 1 (9-inch) pie

340 grams (12 ounces) dairy-free dark chocolate (72% cacao preferred), chopped*

226 grams (1 cup) full-fat coconut milk, whisked until smooth, or heavy cream

3 large eggs (about 150 grams out of the shell), at room temperature**

Cookie Crumb Crust (page 185), made with Paleos

* Weights are given for chocolate because volume measurements are inaccurate. If you don't own a scale, check the chocolate package. It will list the weight on it.

** Forgot to take the eggs out of the refrigerator? No problem! Place the eggs—still in their shells, please—in a bowl of lukewarm water for about 10 minutes before making the pie filling.

Place the chocolate in a high-powered blender. Bring the coconut milk to a boil. (You can do this either in a small, heavy-bottomed saucepan or in the microwave.)

Pour the hot coconut milk over the chocolate. Place the lid on the blender and turn on at medium speed. Blend for 20 seconds or until mixture is smooth. Stop the blender and add the eggs. It's fine to add them all at once. Turn on the blender at medium speed and blend for 90 seconds.

Scrape the filling into the crust. Chill, uncovered, for 4 hours or overnight.

Allow the pie to come to room temperature before serving.

. . . .
Store leftover pie in the refrigerator, wrapped, for up to 3 days.
. . . .

Flaky Pie Crust `coconut-free if made with butter`

Without gluey gluten to hold it together, grain-free pie crust is delicate. This is good news for the eater—the pie crust is super flaky. For the baker, however, it requires a little special handing. You need to roll it out between two pieces of parchment paper and flip it into the pie plate. I like to roll the dough right after I make it. This way, it's a cinch to get it into the pie plate.

Active Time: 30 minutes
Chill Time: at least 2 hours
Yield: 1 single 9-inch pie crust, or 1 double 9-inch pie crust or 2 single crusts

Single Crust

170 grams (1 ½ cups) finely ground almond flour

85 grams (¾ cup) tapioca starch, plus more for shaping and rolling

½ teaspoon salt

85 grams (6 tablespoons) coconut oil or unsalted butter, chilled and cut into 6 pieces

3 tablespoons cold water

Double Crust

340 grams (3 cups) finely ground almond flour

170 grams (1 ½ cups) tapioca starch, plus more for shaping and rolling

1 teaspoon salt

170 grams (¾ cup) coconut oil or unsalted butter, chilled and cut into 12 pieces

90 grams (6 tablespoons) cold water

Whisk the almond flour, tapioca starch, and salt together in a large mixing bowl. Use a pastry cutter or your fingers to cut coconut oil into the dry ingredients until the mixture resembles a coarse meal. You want a few large nubs of coconut oil. If you use your fingers, work in the oil with a quick snapping motion. Add the water and stir with a wooden spoon until the water is incorporated.

Reach into the bowl with clean hands and squeeze the dough into a ball. If the dough is dry and won't hold together in a ball, add an additional tablespoon or two of water and knead it in with your hands.

Dust the counter with tapioca starch. Turn the dough out onto the counter and pat it into a round. If you're making a double crust or 2 single crusts, cut the dough into two equal pieces. Wrap one piece in plastic wrap and refrigerate it for later use.

Place a 12 by 16-inch piece of parchment paper on the counter. Dust the parchment lightly with tapioca starch. Center the dough in the middle of the parchment and dust the top with tapioca starch. Cover with a second piece of parchment. Roll out the dough into a 12-inch circle.

Gently pull away the top piece of parchment paper. Invert a 9-inch pie plate over the center of the dough. Place one hand firmly on the bottom of the pie plate and slide your second hand under the parchment. In one quick motion, flip the dough and pan over. Press the dough down into the pan so it fits snugly. Gently pull the parchment away from the dough. If the dough tears, press it back together. If making 2 single crusts, repeat with remaining dough.

Cover the pie plate with plastic wrap. Chill for 2 hours before filling and baking.

If you're making a double crust pie, allow the dough for the top crust to come to room temperature before rolling it into a 12-inch circle, or the cold coconut oil will make the dough crack. And that's not easy as pie!

. . . .

If you're not using the crust right away, pat the dough into a round and wrap tightly with plastic wrap. Store it in the refrigerator for up to 2 days, or freeze for up to 1 month.

. . . .

Cookie Crumb Crust

There are some pies that just taste better with a cookie crust. For this recipe, select one of the cookies from the list below. Soft cookies, like maple softies, won't work.

Active Time: 10 minutes
Bake Time: 12 minutes
Yield: 1 9-inch pie crust

227 grams (8 ounces) baked and cooled cookies*

3 tablespoons coconut oil or unsalted butter, melted and cooled slightly

2 tablespoons coconut sugar or evaporated cane juice

* Cookies that work for crumb crusts:

Honey Grahamless Crackers (page 115)

Paleos (page 96), unfilled

Gingersnaps (page 100)

Cut-Out Cookies (page 111)

Magic Cut-Out Cookies (page 112), for an egg free crust

Snickerdoodles (page 99)

Adjust an oven rack to the middle position and preheat the oven to 325°F.

Place the cookies in a food processor or high-powered blender and grind to coarse crumbs. Transfer the crumbs to a medium mixing bowl. Add the melted coconut oil and coconut sugar and stir to combine. Press the mixture into a 9-inch pie plate.

Bake until golden brown, about 12 minutes.

Crust should be used the day it's made.

Sweet Treats and Salty Snacks

Chocolate Truffles

Marzipan

Lots-of-Fruit-and-Nuts Chocolate Bark

Nummy Gummies

Maple-Frosted Almonds

Spicy Chipotle Nuts

Roasted Almond Butter

Almond-Ella (Chocolate-Almond Spread)

Coconut Butter

Real, Quick Hot Chocolate

Paris, New York Hot Chocolates

Marzipan, page 190

Chocolate Truffles `almond-free; starch-free`

Active Time: about 1 hour total
Chill Time: 4 hours
Yield: about 40 (1-tablespoon) truffles

113 grams (½ cup) full-fat coconut milk, whisked until smooth, or heavy cream

226 grams (8 ounces) dairy-free dark chocolate (at least 72% cacao)

About ½ cup cocoa powder, natural or Dutch-process, for coating

BAKER'S NOTE: *Chocolate Weights*

Normally I give volume as well as weight measurements. For truffles and other chocolate treats, volume amounts don't work. You really need to use the exact weight of chocolate called for in the recipe. Most chocolate packaging lists both grams and ounces.

Line an 8-inch square or round cake pan with a piece of parchment.

Place the coconut milk in a small, heavy-bottomed saucepan. Heat over medium heat until the coconut milk boils. Turn the heat down to low. Add chocolate and stir with a wooden spoon until smooth. Pour into the prepared pan. Press a piece of plastic wrap directly on the surface of the truffle mixture. Chill for 4 hours, until firm.

Scoop balls (you select the size) out of the set chocolate. Roll the balls between your palms to smooth them, then roll in cocoa powder to coat. Place the coated truffles on a serving tray or into a container.

Store in the refrigerator in an airtight container for up to 3 weeks. Place a piece of waxed paper between the layers to prevent them from sticking together.

Variations

Peppermint Truffles: Add 5 to 8 drops pure peppermint oil along with the chocolate.

Orange Truffles: Add 1 teaspoon orange oil along with the chocolate.

Vanilla Truffles: Add 2 teaspoons vanilla extract along with the chocolate.

Marzipan  coconut-free

If you bake grain-free, you probably have almond flour in the kitchen. So why not make a batch of homemade marzipan? It makes a wonderful holiday gift either plain or dipped in chocolate.

Active Time: about 1 hour
Chill Time: 4 hours
Yield: about 36 bite-size pieces

170 grams (1 ½ cups) finely ground almond flour

226 grams (2 cups) powdered sugar, homemade (page 210) or grain-free store-bought

1 large egg white (about 30 grams)

1 teaspoon vanilla extract

1 teaspoon rosewater (optional)*

* Some marzipan contains rosewater. Since I don't keep a bottle in the house, I skip it. If you happen to have some, add it.

Combine the almond flour, powdered sugar, egg white, and vanilla in a food processor. Run the processor until a ball forms around the blade.

Place a large sheet of plastic wrap on the counter. Turn the marzipan out onto the plastic wrap and pat it into a circle. Wrap well in the plastic wrap. Chill for 4 hours, until the marzipan is very firm.

Lightly dust your counter with powdered sugar. Roll out the marzipan to a 4 by 6-inch rectangle, about ½-inch thick. Cut into bite-size pieces.

. . . .

Store on the counter in an airtight container for up to 3 weeks. Place a piece of waxed paper between the layers to prevent the marzipan from sticking.

. . . .

Variation

Chocolate-Covered Marzipan: Melt 226 grams (8 ounces) dairy-free dark chocolate (72% cacao suggested) (see Baker's Note below). Line a rimmed baking sheet with parchment paper. Spear a piece of marzipan on a fork and dip it in the chocolate. Tap the fork on the edge of the bowl and allow excess chocolate to drip off. Place the dipped marzipan on the baking sheet. Repeat with the remaining marzipan pieces. Chill until firm. Store dipped marzipan in the refrigerator in an airtight container for up to 3 weeks.

BAKER'S NOTE: *How to Melt Chocolate*

Chocolate melts more easily and quickly if it's been chopped instead of left in large pieces. Chips also melt well.

In the Microwave

Place the chocolate in a 2-cup glass measuring cup. Microwave on 80% power for 30 seconds. Remove and stir, even if it doesn't look like the chocolate is melting. (Doing this allows the chocolate to cool a little and prevents "hot spots" that can burn the chocolate.) Repeat in 30-second intervals until the chocolate is melted.

On the Stovetop

Pour about 1 inch water into the bottom of a double boiler. Bring the water to a simmer over medium-high heat. Place the chocolate in the top of a double boiler or a heatproof bowl, and place over (not in) the water. Stir until the chocolate melts.

Don't allow the water in the bottom of the double boiler to boil. You want a gentle simmer; boiling water is too hot.

Lots-of-Fruit-and-Nuts Chocolate Bark `coconut-free; starch-free`

Need a quick and delicious gift? Make a batch of this bark, slide it into a cello bag, tie with a pretty ribbon, and you're done. They get a tasty homemade treat and you get an easy, budget-friendly gift.

Active Time: about 10 minutes
Chill Time: 1 hour
Yield: 1 8-inch square

227 grams (8 ounces) dairy-free dark chocolate, chopped*

55 grams (about ¾ cup) chopped dried fruit (see Baker's Note)

30 grams (about ½ cup) chopped toasted almonds (see Baker's Note)

* 72% cacao makes a lovely bark but use whatever chocolate you love to nibble on.

Line an 8-inch square cake pan with parchment paper.

Melt the chocolate in the microwave (see Baker's Note, page 190). Pour the chocolate into the prepared pan. Use an angled spatula or the back of a spoon to spread the chocolate into a square about 7 by 7 inches. Sprinkle evenly with fruit and nuts. Refrigerate until set, about 1 hour.

Break or cut into chunks with a sharp knife.

. . . .
Store on the counter in an airtight container for up to 2 weeks.
. . . .

BAKER'S NOTE: *Fruits and Nuts*

Dried Fruit

There's no "right" dried fruit to use in this recipe. Any dried fruit works well. In the fall, I like to mix apple rings, cranberries, and pears. In the summer, I'm all about apricots, cherries, and blueberries.

It's often tough to chop dried fruit because it loves to stick to your knife. Instead of chopping it, I cut it into bite-sized pieces with a clean pair of kitchen scissors. For looks, I'll snip some of the fruit into long, thin strips.

Nuts

Toasted almonds are more flavorful than raw almonds. If you are squeezed for time, feel free to skip this step or use store-bought roasted, unsalted almonds.

To toast almonds, spread them in a large dry skillet. Heat over medium-high heat until the almonds are fragrant, stirring frequently. Pour the nuts onto a rimmed baking sheet to cool. When the nuts are cool, chop them into bite-size pieces.

Nummy Gummies

egg-free; almond-free; coconut-free; starch-free

This recipe makes yummy gummy candy. I like to cut out shapes with small cookie cutters, or simply cut the candy into squares. If you want to go for bears and other fun shapes, order some candy molds (see Sources, page 211).

Active Time: about 15 minutes
Chill Time: 4 hours
Yield: about 25 small candies

275 grams (1 ¼ cups) fruit juice*

3 tablespoons granulated gelatin (preferably grass-fed; see Sources, page 211)

113 grams (⅓ cup) honey

2 tablespoons freshly squeezed lemon juice

* Any type of juice works except for pineapple, kiwi, and papaya. These fruits contain an enzyme that prevents gelatin from setting.

Grease an 8-inch pie plate or a candy mold with nonstick cooking spray or brush lightly with melted coconut oil.

Pour ⅔ cup of the juice into a medium mixing bowl, then sprinkle the gelatin on top. Allow to stand for 5 minutes. The mixture will look thick.

Combine the remaining juice, honey, and lemon juice in a small saucepan. Bring to a boil over medium heat, then remove from the heat. Allow to cool for 1 minute.

Pour the juice-honey mixture into the gelatin mixture. Stir until the gelatin dissolves completely. Don't stir too vigorously or you'll create bubbles. Pour the candy base into the prepared pie plate or spoon it into the cavities of the candy mold. Chill for 4 hours, until solid.

Turn out onto a cutting board. Cut into shapes with a small cookie cutter or into squares with a knife.

. . . .
Store in an airtight container in the refrigerator for up to 3 days.
. . . .

Maple-Frosted Almonds `coconut-free; starch-free`

Have you checked out the prices on those little jars of flavored almonds lately? They're pricey! And the high price tag isn't the worst part. Most contain way more sugar than I want. It's easy to make your own, and best of all, you can control the amount of sugar in each batch.

Active Time: 5 minutes
Bake Time: 15 minutes
Yield: 1 ½ cups

227 grams (1 ½ cups) raw almonds

2 tablespoons almond oil* or grapeseed oil

1 ½ tablespoons granulated maple sugar

½ teaspoon kosher salt

* If your diet includes dairy, replace half the almond oil with 1 tablespoon melted unsalted butter.

Adjust an oven rack to the middle position and preheat the oven to 325°F. Line a rimmed baking sheet with parchment paper.

Combine the nuts, almond oil, maple sugar, and salt in a large mixing bowl. Stir to combine.

Spread the nuts in an even layer on the prepared baking sheet. Bake for 10 minutes, then remove the pan from the oven and stir with a metal spatula. This prevents the nuts from burning. Return the pan to the oven and bake until golden brown and aromatic, about 5 minutes more.

Allow the nuts to cool on the pan before transferring them to a serving bowl.

. . . .
Store on the counter in an airtight container for up to 2 weeks.

Variation

Sweet and Spice and Everything Nice. Mix these sweet nuts together with the Spicy Chipotle Nuts on page 198 for a sweet and spicy treat.

Spicy Chipotle Nuts

`coconut-free; starch-free`

When you're in the mood for a spicy, salty snack, make a batch of these nuts. You'll notice a range of amounts for each of the peppers. For mildly spicy nuts, use the smallest amount called for; if you prefer things really hot and spicy, use the larger amount.

Active Time: 5 minutes
Bake Time: 15 minutes
Yield: 1 ½ cups

227 grams (1 ½ cups) raw almonds

2 tablespoons almond oil* or grapeseed oil

1 to 2 teaspoons ground chipotle chile

1 to 1 ½ teaspoons cayenne pepper

½ teaspoon kosher salt

* If your diet includes dairy, replace half the almond oil with 1 tablespoon melted unsalted butter.

Adjust an oven rack to the middle position and pre-heat the oven to 325°F. Line a rimmed baking sheet with parchment paper.

Combine the nuts, oil, ground chipotle, cayenne, and kosher salt in a large mixing bowl. Stir to combine. Spread the nuts in an even layer on the prepared baking sheet. Bake for 10 minutes, then remove the pan from the oven and stir with a metal spatula. This prevents the nuts from burning. Return the pan to the oven and bake until golden brown and aromatic, about 5 minutes more.

Allow the nuts to cool on the pan before transferring them to a serving dish.

Store on the counter in an airtight container for up to 2 weeks.

Roasted Almond Butter

coconut-free; starch-free; egg-free

What's my favorite way to eat almond butter? If I'm honest, I like it straight from a spoon. Of course, it's also good with sliced apples or spread on crackers or a piece of toast.

Roasting the almonds before grinding them into butter makes for a deep, rich flavor. If you are looking for a flavor blast, check out the almond butter variations. From sweet to spicy, there's something for everyone. During the holiday season, I like to give an assortment of flavored almond butters as a gift.

Active Time: 10 minutes
Bake Time: 15 minutes
Yield: about 1 cup

283 grams (2 cups) raw almonds

1 to 2 teaspoons almond oil

Adjust an oven rack to the middle position and preheat the oven to 350°F.

Spread the almonds in an even layer on a rimmed baking sheet. Roast for 10 minutes, then remove the pan from the oven and stir with a metal spatula. This prevents the nuts from burning. Return the pan to the oven and roast until golden brown and aromatic, about 5 minutes more.

Allow the almonds to cool on the pan.

Transfer the almonds to a food processor or high-powered blender. Add the almond oil and blend on medium-high speed until smooth. Spoon the almond butter into a glass jar.

. . . .
Store covered in the refrigerator for up to 2 months.
. . . .

Variations

Maple Almond Butter: Add 3 tablespoons dark maple syrup to the almonds before blending.

Honey Almond Butter: Add 3 tablespoons honey to the almonds before blending.

Cinnamon Almond Butter: Add 1 teaspoon ground cinnamon and 1 teaspoon coconut sugar or evaporated cane juice to the almonds before blending.

Pumpkin Spice Almond Butter: Add 1 teaspoon coconut sugar or evaporated cane juice, 1/2 teaspoon pumpkin pie spice (homemade, page 54, or store-bought), and 1/4 teaspoon vanilla extract to the almonds before blending.

Aztec Chocolate Almond Butter: This butter is less sweet than chocolatey Almond-Ella (following page) and has a nice spicy kick to boot. Add 1 teaspoon natural cocoa powder, 1/4 teaspoon ground cinnamon, and 1/8 teaspoon cayenne pepper to the almonds before blending.

Super Spicy Almond Butter: This savory almond butter makes a great dipping sauce for chicken skewers. Add 1/2 teaspoon cayenne pepper, 1/4 teaspoon chili powder, 1/4 teaspoon smoked paprika, and 1/8 teaspoon salt to the almonds before blending.

Almond-Ella (Chocolate-Almond Spread)

egg-free; coconut-free

My friends love chocolate-hazelnut spread. Since I'm allergic to hazelnuts, I've never eaten it. However, I know a good thing when I hear about it. So I whipped up a batch of chocolate-almond spread. Whoa. Now I know what my friends were raving about!

Active Time: about 30 minutes
Bake Time: 12 minutes
Yield: about 1 cup

283 grams (2 cups) raw almonds

2 tablespoons almond oil

57 grams (½ cup) powdered sugar, homemade (page 210) or grain-free store-bought

36 grams (⅓ cup) cocoa powder, Dutch-process or natural

1 teaspoon vanilla extract

⅛ teaspoon salt

Adjust an oven rack to the middle position and preheat the oven to 350°F.

Spread the almonds in an even layer on a rimmed baking sheet. Bake for 10 minutes, then remove the pan from the oven and stir with a metal spatula. This prevents the nuts from burning. Return the pan to the oven and bake until light golden brown and aromatic, about 2 minutes more.

Allow the nuts to cool completely on the pan.

Transfer the almonds to a food processor or high-powered blender. Add the almond oil and blend on medium-high speed until smooth.

Stop the machine and add the powdered sugar, cocoa powder, almond oil, vanilla, and salt. Blend until combined. Spoon into a glass jar.

Store in the refrigerator in a covered glass jar for up to 1 month.

Variation

Sunflower-Ella: If your diet doesn't include nuts, replace the almonds with an equal amount of sunflower seeds and the almond oil with 2 tablespoons grapeseed oil for a nut-free chocolate spread.

Chocolate Chip Coconut Butter

Coconut Butter `almond-free; starch-free`

My taste buds love coconut butter but my wallet hates the store-bought stuff. Good thing it's so easy to make your own!

To make a smooth butter, you really need a high-powered blender or food processor. And don't confuse coconut butter with coconut oil. Made from the flesh of coconuts, coconut butter is closer to almond butter.

Active Time: 10 minutes if made in a food processor; 5 minutes if made in a high-powered blender.
Yield: about 1 cup

226 grams (2 ⅔ cups) unsweetened dried shredded coconut (sometimes called "desiccated coconut")

28 grams (2 tablespoons) coconut oil, melted and cooled slightly

½ teaspoon salt (optional)

Place coconut, melted coconut oil, and salt in a food processor or high-powered blender. Blend until smooth. In a food processor, this can take up to 10 minutes; in a high-powered blender, it takes about 5 minutes. Transfer the coconut butter to a glass jar.

· ·

Store in the refrigerator in a glass jar for up to 3 weeks.

· ·

Variations

Maple-Vanilla Coconut Butter: For a sweet treat that tastes almost like coconut cake batter, add 3 tablespoons dark maple syrup and 1 teaspoon vanilla extract to the coconut before blending.

Chocolate Chip Coconut Butter: Want to eat chocolate chip cookie dough by the spoonful? This coconut butter lets you do just that! Add 2 tablespoons coconut sugar to the coconut before blending. Stir 42 grams (¼ cup) dairy-free dark chocolate chips (regular or mini) or chopped chocolate into the blended butter. (If your butter comes out of the blender warm, allow it to cool before adding the chocolate chips. You don't want them to melt.)

Real, Quick Hot Chocolate

almond-free, if made with coconut milk; starch-free

The thing about real hot chocolate is that sometimes it's a pain to make. There's a solution: truffles. Make a batch of truffles but scoop them into larger balls. Then when you are in the mood for a mug of real hot chocolate, drop one of the balls into a mug of hot milk. Done!

This recipe was adapted from *Cook's Illustrated.*

Active Time: 10 minutes
Cook Time: 5 minutes
Yield: 20 (2-tablespoon) balls or about 12 (3-table-spoon) balls

Chocolate Truffles (page 189), any flavor, unshaped

226 grams (1 cup) reduced-fat coconut milk* or almond milk for each serving

¼ teaspoon vanilla extract for each serving

* Full-fat coconut milk makes a hot chocolate that's a little too rich to be enjoyed in an 8-ounce serving. For a super rich hot chocolate, see Paris, New York Hot Chocolates (page 209).

Remove the pan of truffle base from the refrigerator and allow it to warm slightly. (This makes it easier to work with.) Scoop into balls of 2 or 3 tablespoons each. Three tablespoons of the truffle mixture makes a deep, rich hot chocolate. For a less-intense hot chocolate, make 2-tablespoon balls. Wrap each ball tightly in plastic wrap and place in a freezer-proof bag or sealed container.

For individual cups of hot chocolate, pour the coconut milk into a microwave-safe mug. Heat until warm, about 90 seconds on high. Drop a chocolate ball into the warm milk and stir. Return the mug to the microwave and heat until the chocolate ball melts and the hot chocolate is warm, about 2 minutes on 80% power. Stir in the vanilla. Enjoy.

· ·
Store the balls in the refrigerator, wrapped, for up to 3 weeks or freeze for up to 6 weeks.
· ·

BAKER'S NOTE: *Hot Chocolate versus Hot Cocoa*

Ever wonder what the difference is between hot chocolate and hot cocoa?

Hot chocolate is made by combining chocolate with hot milk or cream.

Hot cocoa is made by combining cocoa powder with hot milk or cream.

Hot chocolate tastes richer than hot cocoa.

Is one better than the other? Not really. I mean, I prefer the richness and flavor of hot chocolate, but there's also something nice about curling up with a warm mug of hot cocoa.

Paris, New York Hot Chocolates

The first time I visited Paris, I drank a cup of hot chocolate that tasted like warm ganache. I thought of this as a Paris-only treat. Then I walked into City Bakery in New York City on a cold winter day. It seemed like everyone was sipping hot chocolate from tiny cups. I ordered one. It reminded me of what I had in Paris, only this one tasted a little more like warm pudding than chocolate ganache. Here I've recreated both styles. Serve in small 4-ounce portions.

Paris Sipping Hot Chocolate

`almond-free; starch-free`

This tastes like a cup of warm chocolate truffles. It's a rich, thick sipping chocolate.

Active Time: 5 minutes
Cook Time: 5 minutes
Yield: 2 servings

226 grams (1 cup) full-fat coconut milk, whisked until smooth

2 Real, Quick Hot Chocolate balls (either size; page 206)

Pour the coconut milk into a small, heavy-bottomed saucepan. Heat over medium low until bubbles appear at the edges of the pan. Add the chocolate balls and stir until smooth. Divide evenly between two small cups.

New York Hot Chocolate

`almond-free`

When cool, this hot chocolate can be eaten with a spoon. Yup—it's that thick.

Active Time: 5 minutes
Cook Time: 5 minutes
Yield: 2 servings

113 grams (½ cup) full-fat coconut milk, whisked until smooth

1 tablespoon tapioca starch

113 grams (½ cup) reduced-fat coconut milk

2 Real, Quick Hot Chocolate balls (either size; page 206)

Pour the full-fat coconut milk into a small, heavy-bottomed saucepan. Heat over medium-low heat until tiny bubbles begin to appear at the edge of the pan.

Whisk the tapioca starch into the reduced-fat coconut milk. In a slow and steady stream, pour the tapioca-milk mixture into the warm coconut milk. Gently stir to combine. Add the chocolate balls and stir until bubbles appear at the edges of the pan. Divide evenly between two small heatproof glasses. Enjoy warm or cool.

The Homemade Pantry

Grain-Free Baking Powder

almond-free; coconut-free; egg-free

Most commercial baking powders contain a grain-based starch. Thankfully it's easy to make your own. If you'd prefer to buy grain-free baking powder, see Sources (following page) for more information.

Active Time: 2 minutes
Yield: about 6 tablespoons

1/4 cup cream of tartar

2 tablespoons baking soda

1 teaspoon tapioca starch (optional)
   (see Baker's Note)

Whisk the cream of tartar, baking soda, and tapioca starch together in a small bowl.

Store in the pantry in an airtight container for up to 4 weeks.

BAKER'S NOTE: *Starch-Free Baking Powder*

Tapioca starch helps prevent baking powder from clumping. If you want to make starch-free baking powder, go ahead and omit the tapioca starch, just be sure to sift the baking powder to remove any clumps before using.

Grain-Free Powdered Sugar

almond-free

I like to use evaporated cane juice when I make powdered sugar. Its somewhat neutral flavor makes it perfect for frosting and marzipan.

Active Time: 5 minutes
Yield: about 2 cups

170 grams (1 cup) evaporated cane juice or
   coconut sugar

1 tablespoon tapioca starch

Combine the evaporated cane juice and starch in a high-powered blender. Start at low speed and increase the speed until you reach the blender's highest speed. Mix for 30 seconds.

Powdered sugar keeps indefinitely. Store in the pantry in an airtight container.

Sources

Ingredients

Almond Flour

Honeyville
Honeyville.com
1-888-810-3212

Nuts.com (also coconut flour and tapioca starch)
Nuts.com
1-800-558-6887

Baking Powder

Hain Featherweight Baking Powder (contains potato)
HainPureFoods.com

Coconut Flour

Bob's Red Mill (also evaporated cane juice)
BobsRedMill.com
1-800-349-2173

Tropical Traditions
TropicalTraditions.com

Coconut Milk

Aroy-D
Thai-united.com/brands/aroy-d

Golden Star
GoldenStarTrading.com

Coconut Sugar

Madhava Naturally Sweet Organic Coconut Sugar
MadhavaSweeteners.com

Dutch-Process Cocoa Powder

Droste Cocoa
Available at supermarkets nationwide

Evaporated Cane Juice

Wholesome Sweeteners (also powdered sugar)
WholesomeSweeteners.com

Florida Crystals
FloridaCrystals.com

Garlic and Onion (dried, not powder)

Penzeys Spices
Penzeys.com

Gelatin (Grass-Fed)

Great Lakes Unflavored Gelatin
Confectioneryhouse.com

Maple Sugar and Syrup

Dakin Farm
DakinFarm.com

Tapioca Starch

Bob's Red Mill
BobsRedMill.com
1-800-349-2173

Equipment

Candy Molds

Confectionery House
ConfectioneryHouse.com

Food Processor

Cuisinart
Available in stores nationwide

High-Powered Blender

Blendtec
Blendtec.com

Index